Meghan O'Rourke's essays and poems have appeared in the *New Yorker*, the *Nation*, *Best American Poetry* and other publications. She is the author of two books of poems: *Once*, and the award-winning *Halflife*. She lives in Brooklyn, where she grew up.

Praise for *The Long Goodbye*

'Anguished, beautifully written . . . Grief doesn't necessarily make you noble. Sometimes it just makes you crazy, or primitive with fear, and O'Rourke captures that emotional violence with elegant candor'
New York Times

'Meghan O'Rourke has written a beautiful memoir about her loss of a truly irreplaceable mother — yes, it is sad, it is in fact heartrending, but it is many things more: courageous, inspiring, wonderfully intelligent and informed, and an intimate portrait of an American family as well'
Joyce Carol Oates

'In her blazingly honest, relentlessly brave memoir Meghan O'Rourke takes on the strange, impossible time after a parent's death. I couldn't recommend this elegant and fearless book more highly to anyone who has, or who has had, a mother'
Katie Roiphe, author of *Uncommon Arrangements*

'The blend of the lyrical and the journalistic, the personal and the public, shapes this beautifully wrought memoir . . . There is solace to be taken from *The Long Goodbye*, not only because of its delineation of the depths of loss and the possibility of emergence, but because of the beauty of the prose'
Molly McCloskey, *Irish Times*

'Harrowing but intelligently written meditation on bereavement'
Amy Dawson, *Metro*

ALSO BY MEGHAN O'ROURKE

Halflife: Poems
Once

The Long Goodbye

A memoir of grief

MEGHAN O'ROURKE

virago

VIRAGO

First published in Great Britain in 2011 by Virago Press
This paperback edition published in 2012 by Virago Press

First published in the United States in 2011 by Riverhead Books

A CIP catalogue record for this book
is available from the British Library.

ISBN: 978-1-84408-677-1

Printed and bound in Great Britain by Clays Ltd, St Ives plc

Papers used by Virago are from well-managed forests
and other responsible sources.

MIX
Paper from
responsible sources
FSC® C104740

Virago Press
An imprint of
Little, Brown Book Group
100 Victoria Embankment
London EC4Y 0DY

An Hachette UK Company
www.hachette.co.uk

www.virago.co.uk

The Long Goodbye

"O Gilgamesh, where are you wandering?
You cannot find the life you seek:
When the gods created mankind,
For mankind they established death,
Life they kept for themselves.
You, Gilgamesh, let your belly be full,
Keep enjoying yourself, day and night!
Every day make merry,
Dance and play day and night!"

· THE EPIC OF GILGAMESH,
COURTESY OF THE AUTHOR

The bereaved cannot communicate with the unbereaved.

· IRIS MURDOCH

for my brothers and father,

and

in memory of Barbara Kelly O'Rourke

prologue

When I was a girl we visited a town on the banks of the Batten-kill every summer. The cold river cut through a valley in the Green Mountains of Vermont and here the pioneers had stopped and settled, razing the land to make way for corn and cows and building a church and a covered bridge and barns.

We went in June and stayed till September in a cabin owned by friends. At noon we swam in the chill of the river and at dusk we walked through the fields across Route 7 to pick ears of corn under the massing gray clouds. The rows of corn were taller than my brother and I, and I was sure that one day we would be kidnapped by goblins and forced to save ourselves before becoming benevolent rulers of what-ever magic kingdom we'd been transported to. We read books on the porch all afternoon. As night fell my father built a pyramid of charcoal on the grill and lit it and my mother cut vegetables and he opened a bottle of wine and she sat and talked with him while the coals burned down to a fine gray shine. I could hear the sounds of their voices filtered through the screen windows and into the sentences of my book like a prayer. My brother sat on the other side of the couch drawing or reading or singing nonsense songs and sometimes I kicked him to make him sit farther away from me.

We were a family.

I was a child of atheists, but I had an intuition of God. The days seemed created for our worship. There was grass and flowers and clouds. And then there were the words for these things: mare's tails and a mackerel sky, daylilies and lady's slippers and lilacs and hyacinth. There were words even for the weeds: goldenrod and ragweed and Queen Anne's lace. You could feed yourself on the grandeur of the sounds.

I liked to lie on the grass beside the house before dinner, as the sun faded, and watch the twilight overtake the clouds. In the dusk you could see the white clouds move. The first time, I cried out to my mother that I could detect the earth turning. "I don't think so," she said. "That's the wind blowing the clouds." I knew she must be wrong. Lying there on the ground gave me a tickling feeling, as if I might fly up into the sky or sink down into the earth itself.

Each day was holy and lazy and boring. In the mornings I got up and read on the couch in my sleeping bag. The sun would rise and the cloud tips would show over the pines and I would go downstairs with my book to fix a bowl of Raisin Bran. I pretended it was bran mash because I wanted to be a horse. It seemed to me better to be an animal than a human. In those minutes I'd still have the imprint of my mother or my father kissing me good night before turning the light off and I liked to be alone with that feeling of protection in the new day. I liked that protection.

Sometimes, if it wasn't too damp with dew, I called the dog and took a tennis ball and set off up the dirt road to explore. The cabin was on the side of a mountain and there were paths cut into the woods that you could walk. On these paths I would throw the ball far into the underbrush for Finn to chase. I wanted to find out how good a tracker he was. He wouldn't return until he had found the ball. One day I threw the ball so far into a thicket that he didn't come back. At first I could hear him snuffling around and then I could not. I called and called for him and finally turned for home. I thought of him in the anonymous woods searching and refusing to face me until he had done what I had asked of him. He might never come back. My stomach got heavy.

When I got home, I confessed to my mother, feeling ashamed. We took the car to look for him but couldn't find him. "He'll come back," she said, but I knew she was trying to comfort me.

Later, as we sat reading, we heard a crashing in the woods by the house. Out came Finn from the goldenrod, mud-draggled, adorned in prickers, tail high, tennis ball in his mouth. He dropped it, wagging his tail: *Here*. Like a woolen blanket, responsibility settled over me, thick and confining. What I loved wasn't as safe as I thought it was.

Some afternoons we just messed around in the big field by the cabin. I would run into the shoulder-high grasses and Finn would follow me, darting off to sniff at things, turning back to make sure I was OK. One day, as we were out in the field, Finn began circling wildly, paying me no attention. It was some excitement native to his being. The circles got tighter and smaller and then he stopped stock-still, one foot drawn up.

I thought he had gone crazy with epilepsy like our old dog, Puck. I started to cry. (I always thought I was tough, with my tomboyish clothes and bare feet, until something went wrong.) Then three wild turkeys rose ruffling up into the sky. He barked and jumped. When they were high in the air he calmed at last. Finn! I yelled, and swatted him hard behind the ears. I went back to the cabin, dragging him by the chain collar.

I told my mother what had happened.

"I think he might be going crazy like Puck."

"No, sweetie. That's called flushing and pointing," she said, setting the table, her thick black hair wet against her back. "That's what he was bred to do."

When we are learning the world, we know things we cannot say how we know. When we are relearning the world in the aftermath of a loss, we feel things we had almost forgotten, old things, beneath the seat of reason. These memories in me of my mother are almost as deep as the memories that led Finn to flush and point. As the fireflies began to rise one summer evening, my mother called to us. *Look,* she said. *See them? Run and get a jar and a can opener.* And my brother and I ran in for jars and our mother poked holes in the lids and sent us across the lawn to catch the fireflies. The air was the temperature of our skin.

I

love

My mother died of metastatic colorectal cancer shortly before three p.m. on Christmas Day of 2008. I don't know the
exact time of her death, because none of us thought to look
at a clock for a while after she stopped breathing. She was at
home in Connecticut in a hospital bed in the living room with
my father, my two younger brothers, and me. She had been
unconscious for five days. She opened her eyes only when we
moved her, which caused her extreme pain, and so we had
begun to move her less and less, despite cautions from the
hospice nurses about bedsores. A bedsore wasn't going to
kill her.

For several weeks before her death, my mother had experienced confusion from the ammonia that built up in her
brain as her liver began to fail. Yet I am irrationally confident

that she knew what day it was when she died. I believe that she knew we were around her. I believe she chose to die when she did. Christmas was her favorite day of the year. She adored the morning ritual of walking the dogs and making coffee while we waited impatiently for her to be ready; she taught us to open presents slowly, drawing the gift-giving out for hours. On that last day, her bed was in the room where our tree was, and as we opened presents, she made a madrigal of quiet sounds, as if to indicate that she was with us. Her hair was swept up behind her, and she looked like the mother of my earliest memories.

Nothing prepared me for the loss of my mother. Even knowing that she would die did not prepare me. A mother, after all, is your entry into the world. She is the shell in which you divide and become a life. Waking up in a world without her is like waking up in a world without sky: unimaginable. And because my mother was relatively young—fifty-five— I feel robbed of twenty years with her I'd always imagined having.

I know this may sound melodramatic. I know that I am one of the lucky ones. I am an adult; my mother had a good life. We had insurance that allowed us to treat her cancer and to keep her as comfortable as possible before she died. And in the last year of her illness, I got to know my mother as never before. I went with her to the hospital and bought her lunch while she had chemotherapy, searching for juices that wouldn't sting the sores in her mouth. We went to a spiritual doctor who made her sing and passed crystals over her body. We shopped for new clothes together, standing frankly in our underwear in the changing room after years of being shyly polite with our bodies. I crawled into bed with her and stroked her hair when she cried in frustration that she couldn't go to work and apologized for not being a "mother" anymore. I grew to love her in ways I never had. Some of the new intimacy came from finding myself in a caretaking role where, before, I had been the one taken care of. But much of it came from being forced into openness by our sense that time was passing. Every time we had a cup of coffee together (when she was well enough to drink coffee), I thought, against my will: This could be the last time I have coffee with my mother.

Knowing that I was one of the lucky ones didn't make it much easier.

In the months that followed my mother's death, I managed to look like a normal person. I walked down the street; I answered my phone; I brushed my teeth, most of the time. But I was not OK. I was in grief. Nothing seemed important. Daily tasks were exhausting. Dishes piled in the sink, knives crusted with strawberry jam. At one point I did not wash my hair for ten days. I felt that I had abruptly arrived at a terrible, insistent truth about the impermanence of the everyday. Restless and heavily sad, I would walk through my quiet Brooklyn neighborhood at night, looking in the windows of houses decorated with Christmas lights and menorahs, and think that I could more easily imagine myself floating up into the darkness of the night sky than living in one of those rooms like one of those people. *I am a transient in the universe,* I thought. Why had I not known that this was what life really amounted to?

I was not entirely surprised to find that being a mourner was lonely. But I was surprised to discover that I felt lost. In the days following my mother's death, I did not know what I was supposed to do, nor, it seemed, did my friends and colleagues, especially those who had never suffered a similar loss. Some sent flowers but did not call for weeks. One friend launched into fifteen minutes of small talk when she saw me, before asking how I was, as if we had to warm up before diving into the churning, dangerous waters of grief. Others sent worried e-mails a few weeks later, signing off: "I hope you're doing well." It was a kind sentiment, but it made me angry. I was not "doing well." And I found no relief in that worn-out refrain that at least my mother was "no longer suffering."

Mainly, I thought one thing: *My mother is dead, and I want her back.* I wanted her back so intensely that I didn't want to let go.

At least, not yet.

Grief is common, as Hamlet's mother Gertrude brusquely reminds him. We know it exists in our midst. But experiencing it made me suddenly aware of how difficult it is to confront head-on. When we do, it's usually in the form of self-help: we want to heal our grief. We've subscribed to the belief (or pretense) that it happens in five tidy stages: denial, anger, bargaining, depression, and acceptance. (The jaggedness of my experience hardly corresponded to these stages.) As grief has been framed as a psychological process, it has also become a more private one. The rituals of public mourning that once helped channel a person's experience of loss have, by and large, fallen away. Many Americans don't wear black or beat their chests and wail in front of others. We may—I have done it—weep or despair, but we tend to do it alone, in the middle of the night. Although we have become more open about everything from incest to sex addiction, grief remains strangely taboo. In our culture of display, the sadness of death is largely silent.

After my mother's death, I felt the lack of rituals to shape and support my loss. I was not prepared for how hard I would find it to reenter the slipstream of contemporary life, the sphere of constant connectivity, a world ill suited to reflection and daydreaming. I found myself envying my Jewish friends the practice of saying Kaddish, with its ceremonious designation of time each day devoted to remembering the lost person. As I drifted through the hours, I wondered: What does it mean to grieve when we have so few rituals for observing and externalizing loss? What *is* grief?

I am writing here about my grief, of course. I don't pretend that it is universal. Nor do I write about it because I think it was more extreme, more unusual, more special than anyone else's. On the contrary: I believe that my grief was an everyday one.

When we talk about love, we go back to the start, to pinpoint the moment of free fall. But this story is the story of an ending, of death, and it has no beginning. A mother is beyond any notion of a beginning. That's what makes her a mother: you cannot start the story.

But, oh hell, you keep trying.

O NE SATURDAY in May 2006, I took the train to Connecticut to visit my mother. We lived only a couple hours apart, but we hadn't seen each other in months—both of us too busy with work—and I had become vaguely concerned about her. She was having trouble with her knee—suffering from the arthritis that had plagued her mother before her—and her blood pressure was dangerously high. She retained much of the beauty she'd had as a young woman, a beauty particular for its expression of a serenity of soul and a charged wit palpable below her calm surface. But she had gained weight after the birth of my youngest brother, Eamon, when she was thirty-four, and the doctor had asked her to start taking her blood pressure regularly. I worried that she might have a heart attack; she was unusually anxious because she and my father were selling their apartment and leaving behind their old lives in Brooklyn, where they had worked for decades at Saint Ann's, an idiosyncratic private school my brothers and I had all attended; they were moving to Westport to work at a new private school, where my mother had become headmaster and my father, who taught Greek and Latin, was running the language program.

It was a big change. My parents had both worked at Saint Ann's since I was young (my father liked to tell stories of being hired as a barefoot hippie), first as teachers and later as administrators, too. My mother was a person with a strong sense of justice, which made children and teachers alike trust her, and over the years she had been promoted first to principal of the middle school, then to dean of academics; the headmaster had told her that he wanted her to be his successor. Instead, she had made the choice to go to Pierrepont, a school founded a few years earlier by a woman named Isabel, who was ardently devoted to children's education. Charismatic and funny, Isabel had a visionary intensity that my mother found alluring, and she became one of my mother's closest friends. Helping build a new school stimulated my mother's mind as nothing had in years. But it was a stressful job. The logistical challenges—and the sense of responsibility— were enormous, and she and Isabel had to learn how to make decisions together and trust each other. These things weighed on her at times, and inwardly she worried about the future.

You have to try to relax, I would say, when we talked.

That May afternoon was unusually warm. My mother and I went out into the yard of the house my parents were renting and sat by the pool, rolling up our pants and dangling our feet in the cool blue water. Leaning back, she pushed her sunglasses over her hair and turned her face up to the sun. She suddenly looked girlish. As we gazed across the pool at the horses from the farm next door, she talked about the pressures of school and of selling the apartment where she and my dad had lived for twenty years. But mostly she was quiet, content to sit in silence as the early dragonflies skimmed the water. The two golden retrievers, Ringo and Huck, nosed through the grass. Stillness radiated around us. I was happy just to be near her.

A few days later, I felt sick to my stomach and left work early. (I was an editor and writer at *Slate*, an online magazine.) I'd just lain down in bed when the phone rang. It was my mother. "Meg?" her voice rose. "You're home? There's something I want to tell you," she said, with a deliberateness that alarmed me. "And I wanted you to hear it from me." She hesitated. "I haven't been feeling well and I went to the doctor for some tests, and she found a tumor."

"Where?" I said, stupidly.

"In my colon," she continued. "They don't know what it means. It could be benign. They're running tests and we'll know more about it on Tuesday." The way she said, "They don't know what it means," made me hopeful, as if the tumor were something that could be interpreted, like a passage in Shakespeare. It's not a disease; it's a pound of flesh. I could hear that she, too, wanted to think of it this way.

The next week she called as I was walking back from lunch to my office on Fifty-seventh Street. As the afternoon crowd bustled industriously around me, she said, bluntly, "The doctor got the results. The tumor is cancerous." My knees went weak—the cliché is true—and I leaned over the scaffolding beside me, the metal bar hard against my stomach. "I'm going to need to have surgery and then maybe radiation and chemotherapy, and we need to do it soon. But they think they can treat it," she continued.

I do not remember whether I got any work done that afternoon or what, exactly, came next. I remember calling a former colleague and friend who is a cancer researcher for advice. I remember talking to one of my two younger brothers. I remember fighting with my parents on the phone because they scheduled surgery but had done no "research." I couldn't fathom their approach. They didn't know very much about the doctor they'd chosen or whether surgery was even the right course of action. This made me crazy with anxiety and frustration. In my work as a journalist, I collect information for a living. I read books, articles, and studies as a way of knowing the world. I am also a perfectionist. It's cancer, I thought. What if the surgeon is third-rate? We can wait a week to find out more. We need the best surgeon. We need a perfectionist of a surgeon; no, we need *me* to be the surgeon.

M Y BROTHERS, Liam and Eamon, and I spent an inordinate amount of time with our mother when we were children, not only because we went to school where she worked, but because she loved being with kids. She was a bit of a child herself. She had a vivid sense of what makes children feel safe, and she believed in the validity of a child's experience of the world. This is why students trusted her, even when they'd been sent to her office to be disciplined and she was asking them how they could have done something so stupid.

She wasn't a mother who only cared about her kids—we always knew she enjoyed the adult world too much for that—and our house was messy and chaotic as often as not. But she spent hours with my brothers and me making gingerbread houses or sledding or cutting out paper snowflakes. She taught us all to make apple pie, and read *The Black Stallion* to us at night—though she also had a habit of promising to read a book out loud and then giving up partway through. When Eamon came along, I was practically a teenager, and I could see how much pleasure she took in playing silly games with him. Later on, after the three of us had grown up, her best friends' children—Isabel's daughters and our friend Diana's sons—became her stand-in grandkids, and whenever I visited there were still toys in the house.

It's funny what you remember most about a person: after my mom died, we all talked a lot about how much she loved driving. She was deeply at home behind the wheel—a feeling I never understood, since I didn't learn to drive until I was thirty. (She taught me, so I could take her to the doctor.) When Eamon was little, she used to drive him to and from his babysitter's in Brooklyn on her own way to school. Not long ago, I was asking him what he remembered most about her, and he said, "The way she wanted everything to be fun." He reminded me of a game our mother used to like to play: a game of never letting the car come to a full stop on the way home. Sometimes she pressed the gas pedal a bit harder than she should have, and at other times she dawdled, rolling down a block so she'd reach the light just as it turned green, antagonizing the drivers behind her.

She was aggressive in the car. Whenever anyone cut her off or acted wishy-washy (she hated wishy-washy), she'd inevitably honk the horn and, slowly and expressively, say, "You asshole." One morning when she had a meeting, my dad drove my brother to school. Eamon was then about two and a half, with blond curls and long-lashed green eyes. A car cut off my dad. He hit the brakes. Silence. Then, from the backseat, came my brother's lilting voice: *You ath-hole.*

My mother grew up on the Jersey shore, in a large Irish Catholic family, good at merriment, teasing, and storytelling, bad at expressing serious emotions. (Her father died when she was seventeen, and she almost never spoke of him to me.) The oldest of six—there were five girls, and a boy, Sean, whom they all "spoiled"—she was tall, fizzy, and athletic. She looked a little like Ali MacGraw. She showed me a portrait of herself at sixteen, wearing a Western-style shirt, with her thick, shiny black hair parted in the middle and pulled by her shoulders, the sideburns twisted together and slicked in front of her ears in curlicues. "I would spit in my hands and rub it in and pull that hair forward like that," she told me, laughing. "It looked ridiculous." I didn't agree. She was luminous, her dark eyes as open and cool as a horse's. She liked to spend the summers barefoot, taking the bus every day to the beach club, where she swam, or to the Tricorne Farms, where she rode. My earliest memory of my grandmother's house is of studying my mother's riding ribbons pasted up over the den's window—the rich reds and blues, the printed gold lettering (FIRST PLACE), the crimped edges starting to curl.

My mother had me when she was twenty-three; Liam was born two years later. Her youngest sisters were still in high school and college when I was a little girl. I remember them getting ready for dates on Saturday nights, doing their hair and putting on makeup while my mom teased and watched, her long legs crossed, one always jiggling. My aunts used to give me sips of their beer—*Stop that!* my mother would say lightly—and Barbie dolls, and, once, a drag of a cigarette. In their high spirits, I could see the sparkly girl my mother had been, an image that imprinted on me, so that I was, as a child, already nostalgic for *her* youth. (I think I wanted to grow up to be my mother, and it was confusing to me that she already *was* her.) I'd sometimes pretend that I had her life, returning after school to a house with a pool, having friends over to swim, being surrounded by sisters. I tried to write a novel about it when I was thirteen as a way of imagining myself into that world. On warm summer weekends we'd drive out and my parents would put me to bed and then swim in the pool in the dark night, the crickets cheeping. I would peer down through the blinds, watching as my aunts, their boyfriends, and my dad did flips off the diving board, their laughter filling the air.

Growing up as a Catholic had left my mother with a distaste for the Church or any doctrinaire talk of God. It was an antipathy that was a little difficult for me to understand. Raised without religion, I was dreamily attracted to spirituality and rituals. I half believed that there were forces governing my life I couldn't understand. But after my mother made it clear that she thought religion was hogwash—and restrictive hogwash at that—I never talked to her about this feeling.

At her rather unchallenging Catholic school, she was a straight-A student, and she used to tell us that she'd figured out the nuns' system of calling on the class to read; she'd mark her paragraph in advance and then start a new book, secretly. She told us this story to illustrate how good we had it, how lucky we were to live in a city where a subway ride could bring us to the opera, or to a play, or to a museum housing tombs from Egypt. It was important to her that we understood.

THERE IS our mother, and then, suddenly, there is her cancer. It begins with a phone call, a scan, a shock. Disbelief reigns. You distract yourself by watching movies, drinking coffee, doing the normal things. (The night we found out, I played Trivial Pursuit—which my mother had given me for Christmas—with Liam, my boyfriend Jim, and an old friend from graduate school.) The first scan is followed by more scans. In my mother's case, the next scan, in June, was very bad. Colorectal cancer is treatable if it is caught in the early stages. But by Stage 3 the odds of surviving more than five years drop precipitously. By Stage 4—as I had already discovered from the National Cancer Institute website—the survival rate past five years was a mere eight percent. During those first weeks when we were waiting to find out what was happening inside her body, I would lie awake at night praying to an invisible God. *Please, please, please let my mother not be Stage 4,* I whispered. *Anything but Stage 4.*

In June, the PET scan showed that she had more cancerous nodes. "There are two spots on my lungs and one on my liver," she told me on the phone one day. I felt as if I were falling through my chair. She was Stage 4, with metastases to multiple organs. Did she know what this information meant? It meant that she would *probably* die. Should I tell her?

There would be no surgery: the disease had spread too far. Instead, that first summer, she underwent, at New York-Presbyterian Hospital, what her oncologist, Gregory Mears, called "industrial-strength chemo" and radiation. Mears was a calm man, and even though my mother's prospects seemed bleak, he advocated hope: We can't cure it, he said, but we may well be able to turn it into a manageable disease, like diabetes. But I was haunted by the thought of what she was feeling. Was she scared? I could barely formulate the question in my mind. It made me sick. While my mother began her treatments, I spent a lot of time on the porch of a rented house in Long Island with my boyfriend, reading, slapping flies away from my sweating legs, drinking homemade lemonade, trying not to think about it. I was edgy and had difficulty sleeping, and Jim wasn't sure how to help.

My father and I talked every few nights. The news was always bad: My mother was sick, getting sicker, and no one knew if it was the drugs or the cancer or both. I went out to visit three weeks into the chemo and radiation—thinking about it now, I don't know why I hadn't gone sooner—and matters were worse than I'd imagined. The house was filthy. Laundry was piled up on the washing machine. Even the dogs were nervous.

My father had difficulty admitting that he needed help, but his dedication to my mother that first summer touched me. I began to feel a need to batten down the hatches. Jim and I had been together for five years, and while I'd always wanted to have children, I'd never experienced a deep desire to get married. Seeing my mother so ill changed the way I felt. We got engaged at the end of the summer. By August, the combination of radiation and chemo had ravaged my mother. She was barely able to walk, and one night I found her crawling up the stairs, privately, unwilling to tell us how hard it was for her to climb them. But when Jim and I shared our news, her ashen face lit up with joy. "I'm so happy!" she cried. It was the first time she'd looked that way all summer, and within days she started to seem much better; superstitiously I associated the change with our plans to be married.

She had to do one more course of chemo, but when I

visited her at school—she was once again working full-time, having scheduled her treatments on Fridays—she was her usual self: authoritative, wisecracking, in command. Two months later, her doctor gave her the astonishing news: The tests could detect no cancer in her body. This was highly unusual for someone whose cancer had been as advanced as hers. Her remission began, and for a brief time it seemed that all this—the marriage, her illness—was headed in a bright direction.

That winter, my parents moved out of their rental and bought a house in a small town, and I regularly took the train up to visit my mother. Though she'd never been a girly mom, we looked at wedding dresses and visited florists and spent time alone together as we hadn't since I graduated from college. She had always been my protector, but we didn't have the kind of relationship that involved talking every day or sharing every detail of our lives, and I knew she thought I was too anxious, and maybe too preoccupied with work. Over time, too, we had lost some of the ease and physical closeness we'd once had. I missed holding her hand and putting my head on her shoulder—all the loose intimacies of childhood. When I realized how sick she was, I started forcing myself to do these things.

One day, as we shopped for a wedding dress, she sat in the room with me while I took my clothes off. At one point she touched my bare waist and said, "You have a curvy little body, don't you?" In embarrassment, I shied away, saying, "Mom!" I could see our reflections, mother and daughter, diminishing in infinite regression in the three-way mirror, as if we would always be together.

Jim and I were married the following summer at Isabel's house. My mother looked glowing and happy. Near the end of the evening she stood up to speak. "A year ago it didn't look like I would be here," she said. And then she said the thought of the wedding had helped keep her alive. I can't actually remember this part of her toast. But others tell me it's true.

T HREE MONTHS LATER, in October 2007, she had a routine scan. It showed that her cancer had returned. She would have to begin a new round of chemo. That same week I was granted a modest glimmer of what she must have felt. During a routine visit, my gynecologist told me he had found a large "tumor" on my right ovary. It looked, he felt, "highly suspicious." There were characteristics that troubled him. My genetic history also troubled him. It was a Friday; he wanted to perform surgery on Monday.

I walked out of his office, on Fifty-ninth Street, stumbling through traffic and into Central Park. The refrain in my head was banal. How can this be happening to me? I kept saying, over and over. And then: How on earth does my mother bear this? And also: I can't tell her. (I did, but not until I knew a little more.) I had the surgery, a few weeks later, and it turned out my tumor was not cancerous, and my surgery was—though it terrified me—minor. My mother's tumor was cancerous, and her chemotherapy was not minor.

Even today, the divergence in our stories seems like an accident to me. If we went back, I still wonder, could we change the story somehow? Could we take a right turn instead of a left? Seventeen months after her death, I walk through New York and watch the trees bloom once more, and she cannot. I think about how things turned out for each of us, and I recognize that it might be different for me next time. I don't know what story to tell myself about that.

CHAPTER TWO

descent

As it was happening, my mother's decline did not seem inevitable. My mind kept holding out the promise of more time. And the last year of my mother's life was a chaotic one for me. Jim and I separated just eight months after we got married. It is impossible for me to know whether—or to what degree—the separation was an expression of my grief. But when my mother's cancer came back, the differences between Jim and me suddenly became magnified. I found him distant and closed off. It seemed to me that he was having trouble adjusting to being married, let alone being married to someone who was losing all her bearings. At a time when my mother's illness was upending all my assumptions about what I wanted from my life, he was inflexible, locked in his own ways, ambivalent about building a home. He had kept his old apartment as an office, full of his clothes and his kitchen stuff, leaving me with the distinct feeling that our lives were still not bound together. My surgery had given me a fresh apprehension that life is fleeting, and I had a sense of loneliness he couldn't (or didn't want to) penetrate. We fought often, and every failure in communication between us—like our disagreement over whether he ought to take a business trip the day after my surgery—became epic in my eyes. I had gotten married in some way to signal my faith in the future, a future that, I hoped, would include my mother. Once it became clear that our marriage would not save her, I found myself fleeing it. Perhaps I thought I could find something else that would—or some*one* else who could—deliver me from the pain that was heading squarely toward me. In the winter, I went to West Texas on a fellowship, and when I came back I told Jim I wanted a divorce.

Logic might dictate that in the face of my mother's illness I would cling to everything I still had. But I kept doing the opposite. I left my husband. I left my job as an editor, a job that had given shape and structure to my life, to teach and write. I threw myself headlong into an affair with a man who lived across the country, in the Northwest. Even though I knew how sick my mother was, in the summer I went away to be with him, as if I could escape to a life far from home and harm. As I was doing all this, the watcher in me—the part that now and then stepped back and observed my life—thought my actions betrayed how fundamentally irrational human experience is. No one I loved had ever died. Perhaps I believed that if I changed everything, the inevitable would not come, whereas staying put meant acknowledging the awful trajectory we were on. A friend who worked with the terminally ill had told me about what clinicians call "anticipatory grief"— the fact that family members often grieve intensely while waiting for a loved one to die. I thought of my anticipation a lot, picturing it as an invader come to rob me of my joy, a stealthy, quilled creature of the night, a fear that wouldn't let me sit still.

My mother was angry with me because I had left Jim, but wouldn't say it directly. "Are you being reasonable?" she asked when I first told her about the separation, sitting on the back porch, in the spring sun. She sounded chilly and stricken at once. No, I'm not being goddamn reasonable, I wanted to say. You're dying. I'm confused, desperate, despairing. Instead, all I said was, "Why do I need to be reasonable?" And then she shook her head and said, "All I can say is, Hasten slowly, Meg." But I couldn't hasten slowly. I was sick with the speed of time. As Pascal had said, "Not to be mad would amount to another kind of madness."

She didn't see it this way, and that spring, even as she got sicker, we danced around each other. In fact, we barely talked about my personal life. Finally, I called her one day and confronted her. "You insist you're fine," she said coldly, "so why should I ask? You don't want to talk about it." This was true, but it made me angry to hear it. I understood that, facing death, she had wanted me to be settled, and now I had unsettled myself. But the child inside me wanted her to stroke my hair and tell me it would be OK. She didn't, and I couldn't understand why. For the next month, we acted polite around each other, unable to cut through the distance.

In July, I was traveling with the man I was dating when my mother called and asked me to come home for her family's annual barbecue. She was normally loose with us about family obligations, but this time there was an urgent quality to her voice, a note of need that cut through our estrangement. She'd been on a new chemo drug when I left, and for a while that summer had seemed to feel better, her voice light, going swimming every day at Isabel's house. But a recent scan had shown further growth of the tumors in her lungs. Now she sounded sad and private, as if she knew something she wasn't telling any of us. I flew home, getting to Connecticut late at night. My father was up, watching TV in the den, a glass of red wine in his hand; the kitchen was reassuringly disheveled, garlic and onions resting on the island counter as usual. It reminded me of my childhood.

Someone once wrote, "We fear death the way children fear going into the dark." Because my parents were teachers, we had long summer vacations together. For years we stayed in a cabin in Arlington, Vermont. It had two rooms and a dark attic, where Liam and I slept. The first summer we spent there, we had no hot water, and we bathed under a solar camping shower my mother rigged to a tree. Some kind of flying creature inhabited the attic, and I kept telling my parents there was something in the room with us as we slept. Don't be silly, our mother would say. It's OK. I'll leave the stair lights on. But one day as I was moving things around in a dark back corner, an animal whirred past. It was probably just a bird that flew in from outside, my mother said, cheerfully. She must have already suspected it was something else.

The "bird" began appearing at night when we were reading. It moved so quickly you couldn't see it. I had a mortal fear it would touch me, and when it came out, we would scream and clatter downstairs. "Don't be wimps," our parents said. "But why does it just come out at night?" I asked. "It must be a bat!" Liam exclaimed. One night, when my cousins had come to visit, the "bird" got so stirred up it flew down into the living room, where it circled in the light and revealed itself to be a tiny brown bat with pointed wings. Out came the broom; the dog was yapping and leaping, and my brother and I were saying, "We knew it! We knew it was a bat!" Upstairs, I had thought it was going to pull me into the dominion of night once and for all. Down among the lights, and the wine bottles glowing garnet, it seemed small and soft and vulnerable. My father brought the broom down and with a crack got it against the wall. Leave the room, he said, and then he reached down to gather the bat up. Later there were more bats. And I realized it was a family up there, living in our attic.

I mention the story because after I got home that night, while I was talking to my father in the kitchen, my mother came creeping down the stairs in her pajamas. "Meg!" she said, and shuffled over to me. She hugged me and said, "I'm

31

so glad you're home, Meg." She began to cry. "It just makes me happy to see your face."

"I'm glad to be home, Mom," I said.

"No, I'm just so glad," she repeated, as if there were something I hadn't understood, holding me close.

Then she pulled back and looked at me. "I can't believe that when you were a kid we told you the bat in the attic was a bird. I can't believe we made you sleep with the bat. What were we thinking?" she said, and she started laughing and crying, wiping the tears from her eyes. "I was such a bad mother." She was warm in her soft aquamarine nightshirt. I heard the mournful croaking of the frogs outside, and suddenly we were close again. This is how we apologized to each other, and first acknowledged that she was probably going to die.

When I woke the next day it was sunny. I could hear my mother coughing and choking downstairs. The birds were chirping with a pagan intensity, and down the street a lawn mower buzzed, cutting away the summer's growth. It was terrifyingly apparent my mother was having difficulty breathing, but I lay in bed as if listening to a movie. I thought of her black eyelashes, now short from the chemo, her pink mouth, the dark, thick hair she'd had freshly cut. I looked at my tanned legs on the duvet. If I stared at them long enough, it could be any summer, any year—there they were, the same shape as always. Selfishly, I wanted it to be another year, so I wouldn't have to deal with her illness.

I came downstairs. She was in the bathroom by the

kitchen, the door open, kneeling over the toilet. The sounds she was making were harsh. They rasped in her throat like little aliens trying to claw up and out. Of course, the disease is always seen as alien. Never native.

At the family reunion, in New Jersey, we swam in my aunt Jackie's pool and celebrated my grandmother's eightieth birthday with a big buttercream cake. I found it odd to think that my mom's own mother was still alive and well. In the middle of the party my mother took a nap. We woke her up for the birthday ceremony. At the dining table, my grandmother cheerfully blew the candles out, but as we left she looked sad. On the drive there, my mother had girlishly told Liam and me about being awarded the honor pin for "Best Student" in eighth grade at her Catholic school, and how proudly she would wear it on her sweater. "I pinned it on every day," she said, "so everyone could see it."

ADVANCED CANCER makes your appetite unpredictable. That week, after days of not wanting to eat any food at all, my mother wanted to eat chunks of warm, soft Brie left out from the night before. The cheese looked disgusting to me, like something forgotten and ruined—the pale yellow core pooling out beyond the organizing principle of the rind. But she spooned in two bites more avidly than I'd seen her eat anything in months. Her eyelashes were growing back. They were jet black and extremely curly, and they made her look young and a little like a stranger.

Just as my mother's appetite was unpredictable, so were my tastes. I listened to certain songs over and over, singing out loud when I left the house for a run. Songs that used to seem antiquated—"Leaving on a Jet Plane"—now had new textures and qualities. The old words about genuine emotions no longer sounded sentimental or trivial or bankrupt. Over this I had no control. In the face of the future erasure of a specific soul—the erasure of my mother's soul—words about beauty and truth seemed necessary, almost ravishing. So did nature. Earlier that summer, during my time out West, I got a catch in my throat looking at the mountains, with their sublime, gray-purple peaks. In their distances, I saw what Whitman once called "the far horizon fading away," and it spoke to me of the strange change that was to come.

Like a fool, I fell in love with you, I thought, looking at my mom on the couch. But you were always likely to die first.

One day, a good day, we went to Isabel's house and swam in the pool. In the past, when my mother had not been so ill, we had spent many days like this, suspended in cool water, the blue sky overhead, Isabel and her husband Philip's dogs running to and fro, their collars jingling, all of us floating and talking. Isabel and my mother were like teenage girls together: silly and delighted by their silliness, as if it were an iridescent bubble of joy they could step into and stay in forever. "Barb!" Isabel laughed. "Bel!" my mother rejoined. My mother had said something bawdy, something I didn't catch, and shards of their laughter floated up into the air.

. . .

My brothers and I talked around our mother's sickness instead of about it, as if it were safer that way. Eamon was a freshman in college when she was diagnosed. He spent that summer traveling, which brought me a sense of relief: I hated the idea of him seeing how ill she was. Liam witnessed it up close as Eamon and I never did; he worked with my mom and dad at Pierrepont, where he was an English teacher. He had an apartment in Brooklyn but spent many nights in Connecticut during the week. We saw each other a lot in the city, where he lived two blocks from me. I found that I wanted to talk about what was happening, but I could see that he did not. Liam said later that he just wanted to be hopeful, to live in the moment. Eamon was away at college much of the time, but that last summer, before he went back to school, he sat down with my mother to ask her questions about how sick she was. "He wanted to know what kind of cancer it was, what stage it was when it was diagnosed, why I didn't have surgery—all the questions he never asked before," she told me one day after his visit. (I thought of how she and I were different: I would have pressed into everyone's minds just how ill I was.)

I had a different way of dealing: I wanted to "prepare" myself by learning everything, from the start. I read the threads on colorectal cancer websites. I diligently tracked news about the latest studies. My mother had a PET or CT scan every three months, and I waited anxiously for each. I fenced in my terror of the abyss with the pretense that information was control. The man I was dating said, "But the tests aren't the disease. The tests are just tests—don't confuse the two." I realized with a lurch that what he said was true. We would never "know" exactly what was going to happen. This was part of the terror of the disease: the way it turned life into a daily foreboding.

Sometimes I watched my father with my mother, trying to imagine what he felt; he was losing the person he'd lived with since he was young. Unless guests were around, he moved slowly and rarely smiled; he seemed to be holding himself carefully together, afraid he might fly apart. One day, when I backed my mother's car out of the garage, he just watched, in disbelief, as I drove it straight into his car, which was in my blind spot in the middle of the driveway, where he was unloading plants. He didn't wave at me to stop, as if nothing could be done to prevent the collision he saw unfolding before his eyes. But inside the house I found the scattered traces of his solitary caretaking: the pillbox he bought to keep the meds straight, the stacked cases of lemon soda my mother liked.

My mother was getting another scan at the end of the summer, and for a while I hoped that it would show improvement. But after a week or two of being home, I saw that all progress was downward; she was supposed to be designing the teachers' schedules for the fall, but the pain made it hard for her to work for long. One day I understood I had stopped believing that knowledge could save her or help me. I just wanted her to be comfortable. Her pain was mounting. The cancer had spread into the iliac bone in her hip, and it was causing her agony. She tried fentanyl patches, but they made her sick. I called my friend Jerry, a cancer doctor, who said, "Get her more medication. She doesn't need to feel this bad."

So suddenly our mother had a new doctor, a pain specialist who was a hotshot in his field. (His title always made me grimly amused, as I felt I, too, was becoming a pain specialist.) I went with her one day to see him for a checkup of her levels. It was black comedy: She was totally stoned on her meds during the visit. When the doctor and his two fellows came into the room, she told a rambling story about her adolescence. Everyone nodded patiently as if she were making sense. Pacing around, because it hurt to sit still, she began talking about her eating habits and her vomiting patterns. Very liquid, she said. It struck me for the first time that she liked being the center of attention. Listening to her meander, the doctors signaled to me that they would lower the dose of morphine.

Later we saw the radiologist, who advocated waiting and seeing rather than radiating the new tumor in the bone. Shifting on his feet, Dad asked the doctor what would happen six months from now. It broke my heart and made me angry all at once. My mother will be dead, I wanted to say. That's what will happen.

M Y M O T H E R and father had a romance out of a novel. She ran off with him when she was sixteen. He was a teacher at her school; she met him after the nuns confiscated a letter she'd written in class about smoking pot, and threatened to call in her strict Irish Catholic father. What should I do? she asked her friends. Talk to Mr. O'Rourke, the new Greek teacher, they said, he just graduated from college and he's pretty cool. She did. He—swayed perhaps as much by her looks as her case—defended her to the nuns on the grounds that what had happened constituted an invasion of privacy, if not mail fraud. The tactic succeeded. That summer, my mother began studying Greek with my father, but the lessons evolved into the two of them driving around town in my dad's VW Bug and finding quiet places to smoke pot. A few months later, their affair was discovered, and they went off to New York, to the dismay of her parents and his. Her father had always wanted her to go to college, and he decreed that as soon as my mother had been accepted—she was then a high school junior—she could marry my father. He thought his command would put a stop to the romance. Instead, my dad helped my mother take the SAT and apply to Barnard, and she got in. My grandfather died of a heart attack that spring; in the confused aftermath, my mother said she would cancel the wedding, but my grandmother protested. The deal had been made. It was right. My mother should marry my father. And so she did. She was seventeen and he was twenty-three.

In some way she always kept the quality of the youthful bride. She loved animals and gardening. When I was young, she got into photography and began taking pictures of flowers. She was very serious about these photos. She learned about depth of field and apertures and shutter speeds. Soon our photo drawer was full of crystalline pictures of a gardenia blossom or a pale pink magnolia wet with rain. They looked just like the photos of flowers—dew on the petal—used at photo development stores as advertisements. She also loved to bake. My brothers and father and I used to conduct blind taste tests comparing her graham-cracker-crust cheesecake with the famous one from Junior's in Brooklyn. Hers was better, we triumphantly concluded. The Thanksgiving before she died, she tried to make a cheesecake but ended up just wandering around the kitchen pulling pots down and looking at them, saying, "What do I need, what do I need?"

Walking down the street on a day when my stomach wouldn't stop hurting, I told myself that my pain was the pain of a lucky person whose life was about to be touched by the ineluctably real for the first time. I was thirty-two; I shouldn't be so destroyed by what was happening.

And yet this kind of mental calculus had no impact on my limbic system.

WHEN I LEARNED that my mother *was* going to die—nothing to be done, no "therapies" remaining (as if she had exhausted a series of spa options, instead of the chemical frying and steroidal assault she had been under for roughly two years)—I was about to get a massage.

It was a Friday in September. My mother had been given another PET scan, and at noon she was seeing Dr. Mears; I knew that in an hour or two the Call would come. I was waiting in the incense-filled anteroom when the phone rang. *O'Rourke, Home.*

Shit. I'd thought I was going to get this call after the appointment, in privacy; instead I was surrounded by flowers and essences of primrose and girls who feel chi. Was this really the place to learn my mother's fate?

"Meg?" my mother said. She sounded depressed.

She plunged in, no small talk. "So we got the test results back. The cancer has spread into two of my vertebrae as well as the hip bone. And the tumors in the liver and lungs have grown."

"I am so sorry," I said. I sank down on the porch steps, having gotten outside somehow, away from the flowers. But my "sorry" felt a bit like a lie. Did I want my mother to die? No, I did not want my mother to die. But I couldn't stand this pain and sickness. And I couldn't stand trying to comfort her. Mainly, I was in disbelief. I couldn't feel a thing yet—not even sorrow. "Dr. Mears says that there is nothing left to do. There are no other drugs. So we are going to stop treatment now. But he and Susan, my nurse, are going to look into experimental treatments."

"How do you feel?" I asked, not knowing what to say, what my new role was. Was I still her child? Or her supporter? We had not yet moved into our new positions.

"Well, I feel bad," she said, half laughing. Hearing the

disappointment in her voice turned my middle into a lake of curdled pain.

The masseuse was signaling me. "Mom?" I said. "I'm sorry but I have to go. Can I call you later?"

"I have to call Eamon, anyway."

I asked her what she was going to say.

"I don't know. I want him to stay in school. I don't want him to come home. It's his last year in college. He just got cast as the lead in his play. I want him to have that."

"OK," I said. "But . . . but I think he might need to have this, too, to be part of what's going on."

A little door in my mother clicked shut. "Not yet," she said.

"OK."

"Talk to you later," she sighed.

"Yes," I said.

I had gone dead inside. Psychiatrists, I read later, call this "numbing out." When you can't deal with the pain of a situation, you shut down your emotions. I knew I was sad, but I knew it only intellectually. I couldn't feel it yet. It was like when you stay in cold water too long. You know something is off but don't start shivering for ten minutes.

On a hazy October morning a few weeks later, my mother and I drove down to New York-Presbyterian Hospital in the near dark, listening to traffic reports like all the other commuters. We were enrolling her in an experimental treatment program of carboplatin and E7389 run by a Dr. Hershey, whose name brought candy inappropriately to mind. It was a last-ditch effort. I thought, mordantly, that the creeping cars around us were like souls wandering in Hades. My mom was quiet. I worried that she resented my constant fussing about what she was eating and whether my father had given her the right pain medication, but when she called school to check in—as she still did every day—she told her colleague Tundé that she was in the car with her "lovely daughter." Funny how much that meant to me.

Though I'd often picked my mother up after her chemo treatments, I'd never seen one take place. It is a brisk business. Needles and bags are hustled into place with efficiency, as if it were not poison that is about to be put in the body. The nurses were nice, speaking with humor and frankness, though they'd just met my mother. As the drugs slid up the IV into her arm, we watched stolid barges plug up the Hudson like islands, water silver in the haze. I read poems and she asked me about poetry.

"I don't really understand it," she said. "I never have. Do you think you could teach me to read a poem?"

"I do," I said.

That weekend, my friend Karen came to stay with me; I needed distraction. I felt everything had suddenly cracked like a window hit by a baseball, and it was only a matter of time before it caved in, leaving little pieces on the ground. I had just begun teaching two college writing seminars, and working part-time as a coeditor on the launch of a Web magazine backed by *Slate*, and I was telling her about the project. Theoretically I'd be working on it only three days a week, from wherever I wanted. But I was worried about pulling my weight and still being able to help my mother.

Karen and I were talking and window-shopping when my mother called, uncharacteristically weeping. "I need your help, Meg," she said. "I don't know what to do. I feel I am losing my way as a mother." She sounded a little hysterical, like a child. "Just slow down and tell me what happened," I said. "Eamon has been asked to leave Colgate. They found some drugs in his room. I don't know what to do, I can't believe they would do this at a time like this." Then she gathered herself, and sounded like my mother again. "Don't they understand that he's a kid whose mother is"—she paused—"a kid who's going through a really difficult time? I need your help."

"I'll help," I said. "I'll call Eamon, I'll talk to Colgate, we'll figure it all out, it will be OK," I said, too weak not to want to pretend it would be.

"Your father just can't take this right now," she said, a catch in her throat. "He can't. And I just feel confused."

"It's OK," I said, fruitlessly, pushing the hair out of my eyes, "it's going to be OK."

A week later, on a chilly October day, I was having a drink with a friend when my phone rang—

"Meg?" Isabel said, with the special anxiety that nudged my heart to the side.

"What's wrong?" I said. I pictured my mother in the emergency room. I pictured her with blood at her mouth, hemorrhaging from her lungs. She had had her experimental treatment that day. Something must have gone wrong. Or maybe it was my father. I pictured my father—my increasingly gaunt, haunted father—being treated for exhaustion or a stroke.

But Isabel told me that my mother had fallen on her way to treatment and seemed fragile. Could I go up to Connecticut the next day to be with her while everyone was at school?

When I arrived the next morning, my mother was lying in her usual spot on the couch. She looked drawn; she had an afghan at her feet, and the dogs, Huck and Ringo, were beside her. They leapt up, tails wagging, when they saw me, knocking over a glass of water with their large, baffled clumsiness. "Hi, Meg," she called out. Her voice was weak.

I got her some of the San Pellegrino Limonata that she liked. She had mouth sores and wasn't eating much but she still would try lemon yogurt and citrus sodas; the sourness appealed to her. I sat next to her. We talked as I did some work, but she kept drifting off. I wanted to have an unburdening conversation with her. Some part of me was still angry she hadn't been unquestionably on my side during the divorce, and this frustration had come out on the phone the night before; my father and I had argued about Eamon's situation, and my mother had gotten on the phone. Sounding confused, she began to cry and said, "You're both trying to do the right thing. Don't be so mad at each other." I stopped and swallowed (how could I deny my mother this?) and yet selfishly, powerfully, I needed her to know that sometimes we were going to be angry at each other; she had a tendency to want to patch things over before they were ready to be patched up. I hated that she always wanted me to be "reasonable." I wanted her to understand what I felt—it seemed imperative that she should. At the same time, I was haunted by the feeling that my divorce had given her one more cause for worry, and I wanted to know, once again, that I had her love and forgiveness. But she kept slipping into a half-focus. Ringo came over and wedged himself between the coffee table and my legs, his tail nearly knocking over my tea.

"Why must he always do that?" I complained. My mother opened her eyes and laughed.

"It's true," she said, bemused. "I mean, why doesn't he just go under the coffee table?"

"I don't know," I said slowly. This was when I knew something was not right.

The coffee table extended almost to the ground. The dog was a golden retriever. There was no way he could fit in the inch or so under the table. Several times over the past two weeks my mother would forget a word and say to one of us, "I can't believe I don't know that word!" Or she would say, "I don't want to take so much Percocet, I am having a hard time remembering things." The day before, she'd inexplicably taken a thousand dollars out of the bank. "Your father was so annoyed," she told me. "I don't understand why. I just got confused."

And a week earlier she'd complained that her ear was buzzing.

I called the nurse coordinating the experimental treatment, who mentioned I'd made an appointment for the wrong day. "Didn't your mother tell you it had to be Thursday?" she said. "I just told her."

"That's odd. She normally would remember that kind of thing." I paused. "To be honest, she seems confused."

"Confused?" the nurse said. "Or forgetful? I noticed last time she was here she was forgetting words. But that is common when you're taking as much pain medicine as she is."

"I don't know," I said, frustrated. "What is the clinical difference between confusion and forgetfulness?"

"Confusion means she doesn't understand things, or makes mistakes that don't have to do with memory."

"Well, she seems *confused*," I reiterated. "And she fell yesterday."

"Probably it's just forgetfulness," the nurse said, too blithely for my taste.

"What are the chances she could have a brain tumor? She seems . . . off," I said.

"I don't think she would have a brain tumor with colorectal cancer," the nurse said. "It wouldn't present this way. But I will check with Dr. Hershey."

I was standing in the laundry room with the door closed

so my mom would not hear me discussing her symptoms. Her dirty shirts were piled on top of the washing machine.

The nurse called back. "The doctor thinks you should go to the emergency room."

"What?"

"He agrees that a tumor wouldn't present this way, but you should check it out. She could have ammonia buildup in her brain due to the tumors in her liver. That would cause confusion."

I was getting angry. I had no idea what to do. My mother ran a school, for Christ's sake. She was the boss of many people. She didn't like to be taken care of.

I went downstairs slowly.

"Where've you been?" she said, eating tomato soup I'd brought for her. I sat down next to her and took her hand.

"Mom," I said. "I don't want you to be upset." She gave me a funny look. "But when I got here I noticed you seemed a little confused. I asked the nurse about it. And she and Dr. Hershey think you should go to the emergency room. So I think we should go. Is that OK?"

"The EMERGENCY ROOM?" she said, in shock. "Why?"

"They're concerned that there might be some ammonia building up in your brain. They also want you to have an MRI just to check everything out and make sure it's all OK."

This was awful. Somehow I was the person telling my mother that things were getting bad. That we were now in ER territory. To me this seemed a dangerous new place, a

Siberia it would take weeks to cross. No: a Siberia we'd be stuck in for good. Surely they were wrong. She just needed to sit, to rest—

What was I thinking? She was terminally ill. We all knew this was coming. Why had I thought it would be different?

"But I just had an MRI," she said.

"When?"

"When I had shingles."

"But you had shingles last year," I said.

"No I didn't—I just had them."

"That was last fall, Mom. It was after my wedding."

"I KNOW," she said. But she looked confused. Because she *was* confused. She sat quietly. Then she looked up and said, "Well, I *have* been having some strange symptoms. I was telling your father about them. And he kept insisting it was the medicine. But I didn't know why the medicine would do this."

"Like what?"

"Like, I would be sitting here looking at the TV with him. And one night I felt like the TV should be over *there*"—she pointed toward the hallway corner—"like it really *was* there and the image was just projected here."

"Hmm."

"And today Isabel was making an appointment for the blood work for me, and I couldn't remember what day was what."

"You mean *I* was making the appointment for you?"

"No, Isabel. She brought me soup and—"

"Oh," I said. "OK. Get your coat on, Mom, it's time to go."

I called my dad and Liam, who were on the way home, and waited for my mother downstairs. I derived a strange comfort from being able to take her to the hospital. Liam got to see her every day at school. He and she had the same sense of humor. In the face of her pain, he and Eamon both knew how to make her laugh. I could only ask how she felt, or drive her to and fro.

Where was she?

"Mom!" I shouted and bounded up the stairs. She was drifting along putting clothes away.

I'd insisted that her doctor call the ER ahead of time, so we were whisked into triage like VIPs. When the nurse asked Mom questions, she gave answers that weren't accurate. I shifted to and fro and made faces. How do you interrupt your mother and tell her she is losing her grip on reality? By just doing it. Inside, the nurses gave her a private "room"—a nook, really—and handed her a lime-green gown. The entire ER was coated in green. All the nurses wore green "animal" scrubs. One nurse's were papered with pastel fish, another's with rabbits. We are not *children*, I thought. "Now open your mouth," the nurse said to my mom, in an enticing voice. "Dr. Popper will be with you in a moment."

Outside our nook, a frail, white-haired woman who must have been in her eighties lay on a stretcher moaning. I stared rudely. There were nurses everywhere, but no one was paying any attention to her. Evidently, she'd been seen and was now in the purgatory of Waiting for the Next Step, whatever that was. We had entered the country of bureaucratic confusion, a hub plastic and colorful and empty as the innards of a Tinkertoy. "AHHHHOOW," the woman went. It sounded oddly—and obscenely—like an orgasm. My mother looked over appraisingly. "They better give her more of whatever they're giving her."

Machines buzzed and clicked around us. Hell, I thought bitterly, was technology in the presence of inevitable death. Because the machines were present, no one—no *person*, that is—seemed to feel the need to be, unless we made them pay attention to us. I understood the power dynamics here—I was not supposed to ask too much, not supposed to know too much. To try to assert authority would only mean you'd be met with lassitude. Instead, you had to coax their help by deferring to the charts, the information. Meanwhile, they wore animal pajamas and gave you animal clothes, like you were all in a twisted episode of *Romper Room*. It was the stupidest thing I had ever seen.

I asked my mom if she was hungry. She nodded. Why don't I get you a yogurt? I said, and I headed upstairs, back to normal life, where people were in the hospital for routine procedures, bearing children and having tonsils out and eating ice cream, getting flowers and going home.

When I came back, my mother was in her aqua gown and socks. She dutifully told me they had taken her in for the MRI. I opened the yogurt and gave it to her. I had forgotten to get her a spoon, so she drank it. I paced, pulling the curtain back to search for Dr. Popper and his Information. Sirens went off outside and one of the nurses—this one in ducks—said to a tall doctor running past, "Do we have a trauma here?" I heard a short laugh behind me. My mother was pointing at her nose, on which a dab of bright yellow lemon yogurt sat. "Look!" she said, in high amusement. "I'm like a child."

An hour later, as my mother dozed, the ER doctor flicked the curtain back to enter. His balding head was down, looking at a scan. "So, wow, she does have nodes on the brain after all," he said without affect. "I'm gonna call Dr. Chi, the oncologist upstairs, to come take a look." Then, barely looking at either of us, he turned to leave.

My mother was staring blankly. "Dr. Popper," I broke in, "so you mean my mother does in fact have tumors in her brain?"

"Yeah," he said. "Two over on the left side. They would be in a place that's consistent with the spatial confusion you've been describing. Very unusual. So I'll get Dr. Chi."

Silence. The noises and clicks continued. I didn't want to look at my mom; I couldn't bear what I was going to see in her eyes. Then she said, as if she were telling a joke, "Well, THAT was awfully casual of him!"

I could hear the effort in her voice and it broke my heart. It was easier later, when she got irritated and said, "He's just talking to you. He's got to stop doing that. I'm here, too. *I'm* the patient."

. . .

I called Dr. Hershey, the new research oncologist. For all my mother's hard-won lightness, I was furious. How could none of the doctors have warned us? A man picked up. "Dr. Hershey here." "Oh, Dr. Hershey," I said, faltering. Then I felt pleased: I could tell him what happened; I could make him feel remorse for his ignorance and punish him with my prescience. *I* had known she had tumors. *He* had not.

"This is Meghan, Barbara's daughter. We called today, because she was experiencing confusion, and your office recommended she come to the ER for tests and scans."

"Yes, yes—how is she doing?"

"Well, actually, the MRI shows she has several lesions on the right lobe of her brain. It looks like the cancer has spread to the brain, in fact."

Pause.

"*Real*-ly," he said slowly. His response was dramatic. But his tone was not the one I had hoped for. He didn't sound embarrassed or apologetic. Instead, he sounded *intrigued*. "That's highly unusual," he drawled.

Then, gathering himself, he said, "I'm sorry to be clinical about it. I know this is your mother, but that is fascinating. This rarely happens with colorectal cancer." Another pause. "And you've been dealing with this long enough now that you have a sense of what is taking place."

"Yes," I said, stunned into monosyllables by his assumption that I could think clinically about the fact that renegade cells were devouring my mother from the inside out.

"I mean, when I was a boy, OK, not a boy, but a long time ago, you read the clinical lit, there was nothing about mets to the brain. But that's because so few people make it as long as your mother. She's an outlier. She's rare. We're learning things about the disease from her and people like her. We have seen this type of development, but almost never. In the past, patients with her diagnosis would never have lived this long. We used to think it went just to the lungs and liver, and not to the brain—unlike say, breast cancer."

"Right," I said.

"Well, I am sorry to hear the news."

I gathered myself. "I'm calling to see if we can take her home. I'd prefer not to leave her here in the hospital overnight, as you might understand."

"Yes, that should be fine. They'll probably give you some steroids to reduce the swelling around the lesions, and discuss surgery options. Give us a call tomorrow."

But he didn't say that this new development would mean the end of her experimental therapy, which left me a ray of hope—like the sliver of light as a door is closing. I got off the phone allowing myself to think that after this surgery, she'd be mentally tip-top again. And then she could go back to the therapy. And perhaps the therapy would work, and six months from now she would be running the school once more and being my mother, taking care of things.

She was released that night, after another doctor delivered the good news: The tumors were "operable" through radiation surgery. It was cold and rainy outside and I bundled her in a warm scarf and walked in front of her to protect her from the wind. My father had ordered pizza, and when we got home we sat in the den and ate while she lay on the sectional where she always lay. The dogs nosed around my feet and wagged their tails. Liam told her funny stories about school. It felt strangely normal, part of a life that had vanished some time ago.

But the next day the liaison called to say my mother would no longer be part of the experimental treatment. She would be discontinued. Like a TV show? I think. Is this how it works? *Sorry, no one was watching that show, so we have discontinued it.*

It was up to us now. Only we believed.

What did we believe?

The options had dried up. No one had actually said the words yet: Your mother is going to die. And yet our mother was going to die. We were clinging, for the moment, to the possibility that the radiation surgery would make her better, even if only temporarily. It was another thing to do, another way not to talk about that thing growing inside her, invading her bones like little rotten spots on a vegetable, all soft and dark.

I am still looking for the alternative outcome to this part of the story—as if had I pushed harder at one of these moments, had I been more aware, all would have changed. Choose Your Own Adventures were a fad when I was a kid. I had a sense of special providence, and if, reading a story I liked, I made a bad choice, I would pretend it hadn't actually happened. I had, in essence, to lie to myself about my own poor outcomes. This was what I was doing then and it is what I am still doing, rummaging through the bric-a-brac of my mind for possible alternatives, the family silver that was put aside in the attic but still gleams unseen in the autumn sun.

CHAPTER THREE

the particulars

If the condition of grief is nearly universal, its transactions are exquisitely personal. My grief, I know, has been shaped by the particular person my mother was to me, and by the fact that she died at fifty-five. Then, too, I was bound up with her in ways that stretched beyond our relationship: I live a mile from where I grew up, in a neighborhood in Brooklyn where, when I walk down the street, I always see a store or a house that reminds me of her.

I'm not sure that I buy this, but psychologists theorize that grief is sometimes connected to your general level of anxiety and the kind of attachments—secure, insecure, avoidant, ambivalent—you have to others. My anxiety level has always been high. As a toddler, I hated the feeling that my socks were wrinkling under my feet, and in the morning would ask my parents to take my shoes off and put them on over and over until I felt my socks were not, as I put it, "scrabbled." The world frightened me: when there was lightning outside my window, I took it personally. It seemed that everything was here only to be lost. The world was beautiful and it would be taken from me; I would die, and so would everything I loved. People seemed loud, drunk, violent, unpredictable. (Of course, it was the 1970s, and in many ways they were.)

I adored my mother, but I also thought, as a teenager, that I was closer in temperament to my father—an Egyptologist, who, in addition to teaching, worked part-time at the Brooklyn Museum and who, I sometimes like to joke when I'm mad, can speak every dead language and none of the living. When we were children, he was a conjurer and storyteller, the one who could tell you what card you were going to pull from the deck, the one who recounted extravagant five-minute jokes, his wild red hair standing out around his head. But beneath the bonhomie, he was anxious, too, beholden to routine— perhaps why he studies ancient cultures and painstakingly translates old texts. Whenever my brothers and I wanted to take a trip somewhere new, we would plead with my mother; she would turn to my father and he would say, "What's wrong with Vermont?" My mother was more even-keeled and, as my father later put it, always present.

And yet she could be demanding of us, and sometimes I thought she was hardest on me, since I was the oldest child and the only girl. She and I occasionally clashed subtly. One way to put it would be to say I was nervous and my mother wasn't, and sometimes my neuroses were difficult for her.

I was a picky eater, yet she would insist that I eat what was on my plate. I would slip into my bedroom and sulk, hungry but unable to comply. Eventually, she would cave and come in with a sandwich. The standoff usually lasted an hour or more, during which period I hated her. (Or, as a motherless little girl writes to her grandmother in Tove Jansson's novel *The Summer Book*: "I hate you. With warm personal wishes, Sophia.") There was nothing special about those fights except that I was so thin-skinned that they translated for me into the potent suspicion that my mother and I were profoundly different from each other.

I was a secretive child. I remember once looking up from an elaborate imaginative game in my notebook at my brother, who was playing with horses and trucks out loud as my mother and father walked through the room. This horrified me; when I played alone, I played in my head. And yet for years my mother was able to see into my head; she was the person who lightened its occasional darkness. (It makes a strange sense that whenever I got uptight or impatient, she would say, "Lighten up, Meg.") When I was in first grade, my class put on a play about the myth of Finn M'Coul, the Irish hero who battles the warrior Cuchulain. I was excited until I got cast in the role of Cuchulain. For reasons now obscure to me, I was embarrassed by the idea of playing a boy in front of the class and our parents. I didn't know what to do. It seemed so awful that I couldn't even mention it. Instead, I nursed my shame in private, thinking that something would keep it from happening. The day before the play, I couldn't eat anything. I pushed the food around on my plate. My mother gave me a look. At bedtime, the panic worsened. I lay in the dark and wept quietly. Somehow—and how I don't know—my mother heard me. She came in the room in her bathrobe and pushed the hair away from my forehead and said, "Sweetie, what's wrong?" I wouldn't answer. She quietly said, "Whatever it is cannot be as bad as you think." Somehow this sentence unlocked me and I confessed. She smiled. "Honey, no one is going to care. You're not really a boy. It's acting." When my mother said it, in the dark, in her nubbly maroon bathrobe, I believed her fully, as I would have believed no one else, and I relaxed as she stroked my hair and shushed me to sleep.

Whenever I inwardly berated myself about some failing, my mother was the one who knew best how to pull me out of my self-assault. Often she was the only one who noticed. To this day, when I am struggling with a difficult task, I pace my apartment feeling off-kilter, thinking, *I need something; what is it?* And I realize: my mother. She had, as my father put it, a clear compass. Once, in the eighth grade, instead of going to a chaste slumber party at our classmate Carly's, my friends and I sneaked out with some boys to see *The Rocky Horror Picture Show*, and a couple of days later one of the boys I'd gone with told on me after getting kicked out of class, in the hope of distracting my mother from his antics. When I walked by her office, she crooked her finger at me. "You," she said, from behind her desk. "Yes, you, Meghan, you're not going anywhere till I talk to you." I went in, tears of guilt already springing to my eyes. But she just looked at me and said, "Meg, you need some better friends." I stiffened. She said, "*The Rocky Horror Picture Show*, hmm? It's OK. But find some friends who don't rat you out afterward." And then she said, "Now get out of my sight, sweetheart, and don't lie to me again."

I thought of my mother as more natively relaxed and outgoing than I was. But every so often something would happen that would make me realize we were more similar than I'd thought—my mother would idly say how shy she'd been when she moved to New York, and met my father's friends. I remember how nervous she was when she had to speak in public for the first time, at a school meeting just after she'd become head of the middle school at Saint Ann's. (She must have been the same age I am now.) She fretted all that morning, dressing. I agonized with her, because I was deeply shy, and such a task seemed heart-freezingly frightening. Afterward I asked her how it went. She said, "You know, you just have to do it. You don't have a choice. And then once you've done it, you can do it again, and it isn't so bad." She was a pragmatist at core: if you could be present, intensely present, the rest would work itself out. Later I realized that this was much harder than it looked.

Once when I was in college, my parents had a dinner party with some teachers. It was a festive midwinter affair and everyone got a little lit on red wine. As two young teachers were talking past us, my mother leaned over to me and said, "I just wrote my mother a letter about what she meant to me. We're bad at saying these things in my family, but she's getting older and I wanted her to know. And it made me think about you, and how there are so many things I don't say to you, but I want you to know." What she said next was just that she loved me and was proud of me, but those words, prefaced by

61

her sharing a piece of her experience of what it was like for her to be in the world, meant much more than the same words in any other context. I recall clearly the sensation I had—a squeezing, falling one, a silly, encompassing flush of love. And also this: In that moment I could see her as more than my mother; I could see her as a daughter, a person who'd had to make her own way, who'd had to learn to speak in public, to command authority—things she did now with such ease you'd never guess that once they struck her nearly mute with fear.

And so as I write this, I am hit by a feeling of error, a sense that during my twenties, when I thought my mother never quite understood me, it was I who saw her incompletely. I remember the times when she filled my Christmas stockings with the hand warmers sold in ski shops, so I could make it through the winter with warm fingers. (Who would do that for me today?) I took for granted so many of her seemingly casual qualities. The familiar old panic rises in my stomach. "Don't worry about that, Meg," Isabel tells me, when I say as much to her one night before my birthday. "It wasn't your job to tell her she was a great mother. It was her job to be your mother."

O F MY MANY ANXIETIES, the one I was most secretive about was my fear of death. It seemed impossible to confess. One cool summer day, curled up in my sleeping bag on the couch, reading an Agatha Christie mystery, I listened as my brother Liam, fiddling with the radio dial while my mother dealt a hand of Go Fish, turned to her and said, "I don't want to die. Do you not want to die? What happens to us when we die?"

And my mother put the cards down and said, slowly, "No, I don't want to die. But I don't know what happens to us when we die."

"It's scary," he said.

"Yes, it is," our mother said, calmly. "But it's not going to happen to you for a long time."

I was nauseated and riveted: these were the words I wanted to say, and could not say—the comfort I wanted to seek in her, only her, and could not seek. Perhaps that is because I already felt that any comfort she could offer would be false. Dismayingly, this problem was one that she could not solve.

CHAPTER FOUR

anticipation

So much of dealing with a disease is waiting. Waiting for appointments, for tests, for "procedures." And waiting, more broadly, for *it*—for the thing itself, for the other shoe to drop. Except in the waiting you keep forgetting that "it" will really happen—it's more like a threat, an anxiety: *Will my love love me forever?* My mother couldn't have her radiation surgery (called CyberKnife) on the nodules in her brain until after Thanksgiving. So we waited. Her confusion was getting worse. She couldn't go to school and she couldn't be alone.

One day, my father drove to upstate New York to pick up Eamon from college. My brother had appealed his suspension, but the school had rejected it, which meant he had to come home. Our friend Diana was with my mother, and I came up to relieve her. Diana, one of my mother's closest friends, had been my father's student at Saint Ann's many years earlier. She babysat Liam and me back when my parents used to go on "date night" every Tuesday. We liked these nights, because Diana was the funniest of all our babysitters; with her mellow and bemused approach to chaos, she reminded me a bit of our mom. After college, she became my mother's assistant, when my mom was appointed head of the middle school; later, my mother promoted her to assistant head. They were a Laurel & Hardyish pair, always teasing and playing and joking. Now Diana regularly visited, to see my mom and to help out when my dad couldn't be there.

Diana was trying to make breakfast, but my mother couldn't focus long enough to decide what she wanted. Then she would get frustrated and insist, "Don't worry about me. . . ."

She had the choosiness of a fussy toddler, complicated by the pride of an adult. Finally Diana just made her eggs, and my mother pushed them away and said, "No, you eat them, I'll make some for myself."

"But these are for *you*," Diana finally said, slight frustration entering her voice.

My mother heard it, pulled herself up, and put on the jokey face she had developed for these moments, to make things she'd done in confusion seem like little pranks. It was her way of having a modicum of control. "Of course they are!" she said brightly, and began to eat.

Later she turned to Diana and said, deliberately, as if she could find words that would burn through the fog in her mind, "You know, sometimes I have this feeling that I just want to . . . *pop!* Do you know that feeling? I just want to pop."

Diana had to turn away to hide her face.

A week later my father, my mother, and I were sitting in the living room, discussing how my mother would get to a doctor's appointment. She kept insisting she could drive herself. "I'll be fine," she declared.

"You can't drive, Mom. I'll drive you," I said. My father and I began squabbling about the particulars. I was annoyed that he wasn't doing it. He seemed to have trouble going to the hospital, and his resistance infuriated me. Why wouldn't he just take the day off from work? He told me to stop being so bossy.

"Stop it, you two," my mother said, using the look she gave her misbehaving students, a look Eamon called "the Skeleton Face."

My dad left the room. He came back a few minutes later with his fist closed. "Time to take your medicine," he said to my mother. She tapped his fist and he opened it: there lay five pieces of candy corn, left over from Halloween.

"Well, thank you!" she said, a smile flickering.

"Mom," I said.

"Mmm?" she said. She was staring into space, as if seeing something that was not there.

"Are you hungry?"

She turned her eyes toward me. "Mmm," she said. Silence. Minutes went by.

"Mom!" I said again.

"Mmm?"

"Are you hungry?"

She hunched herself up a bit. She was tangled in an afghan and in the nodes of the TENS machine I had bought her a few weeks earlier from a dismal medical supplies store in Norwalk; it provides electrostimulation to the nerves and helps diminish local pain (in this case, from the tumor in her iliac bone). "I guess I should be," she said.

"What do you want?"

A blank stare. Her stomach was showing; her pants were too big. When I had come downstairs that morning, she was in the kitchen, putting cups away into odd places with one hand, and with the other she was holding a tape measure around her waist, as if it were a belt.

"I don't know," she said blankly. "Maybe . . . some yogurt?

"OK," I said. "You need to drink something. Water? Juice? Limonata?"

"Limonata," she said.

She looked at me puzzled where I stood in the doorway. "Shouldn't you be standing over there?" she said, pointing to a chair in the corner. "I look at you and I think you should be standing there."

I realize now as I write that my memories are blurring. Which trip was which? How did I get there the second time? I had been sleeping poorly, and I was exhausted. Trying to teach two college writing seminars and work on the website and have a relationship and help with my mother: none of it was working. I was spending a lot of time in Connecticut, and I was moody and terrified, and inevitably matters had frayed in my romantic life. At one point the man I was dating said, You're choosing your mother over me. I hadn't seen it as a choice. A few days before Thanksgiving, I found out that my divorce had been finalized; holding the official certificate, which had arrived in the mail, I went heavy with loneliness. I quickly filed it in a manila folder, so I didn't have to look at it. I was counting the days until my mother would have the radiation surgery on her brain. I already missed her. I was irrevocably aware that the Person Who Loved Me Most in the World was about to be dead.

Of course, I had my father, too. But fathers love in different ways than mothers do.

On Thanksgiving Day, I drove to my parents', where we were all going to have dinner with Diana and her husband, Josh, and their three boys. I had my mother's car, which I'd borrowed a week earlier, to help me get to and from Connecticut. I was happy to be driving home, but I was wrung out. My relationship had come to a crashing halt. The night before, the man I was dating had called one final time, and we had fought, and he had enumerated my failings, and I had been up all night examining my motives.

And because I had indeed told lies, and had kept secrets, I found truth in many of his accusations. I was losing my grip. My mother was dying, and the only person I wanted to talk to about my despair over it was *her*.

After a long trip, I opened the door to the smell of turkey and pie and thought: *I still have a home.* "Hello!" I cried out. Inside, Diana and my mother were chopping vegetables. For a moment everything seemed comfortingly familiar.

But my mother's hair was messy and tangled and she waved hello absently. She was shuffling oddly, perhaps because of the pain from the tumors in her spine, and her pants drooped around her hips. When I gave her a kiss she only half responded, as if some part of her maternal brain were simply no longer present. My father, meanwhile, was stretched out on the couch, looking bleary-eyed and feverish. He didn't even say hello. (The next day, we would discover that he had pneumonia and shingles, as if the universe wished to add insult to injury.)

I busied myself unpacking groceries when I heard my mother shuffle toward me. "Meg," she said, bitterly. "There's bird shit on the car." Diana shot me a glance—a sympathetic, oh-no glance.

"Oh," I said. "I'm sorry."

"That is *very* bad for the car," she said.

"OK," I said. "I'll get it washed."

"It eats away at the veneer, it's very bad."

"Mom!" I snapped, wheeling around. "I know. There is nothing I can do about it now—I'll take it to be cleaned tomorrow."

She rolled her eyes and walked away. I joined Diana and, pretending nothing happened, began washing the apples for the pie; as we talked, my mother shuffled over to the kitchen sink. She picked up a sponge, dumped dish soap on it. *Shuffle shuffle,* toward the garage door. Diana raised an eyebrow.

Exit cancer-riddled mother to wash car with sponge.

It might have seemed amusing if it hadn't been so damn awful.

"Mom!" I shouted. "What are you doing?"

"I am cleaning the bird shit off the car," she said acerbically. She meant clearly: *You are favored no more, my daughter.*

I felt I was losing my mind.

"Don't do that," I said. *Shuffle shuffle.*

I followed her into the garage; she was bent over the car, fruitlessly swiping at the encrusted bird shit with the fucking sponge.

"Mom, don't do that," I snapped. "I'll have it cleaned tomorrow."

Bending down, she muttered about the wax and the bird shit eating away at the wax; in confusion, I retreated to the kitchen. She came back in the house. "Are you upset with me?" she said. "Are you upset about something?"

When I got angry as a kid I would hide in my bedroom and get under my quilt and cry till I was too hot and sweaty to stay under it anymore. The quilt was yellow, patterned with dark yellow butterflies. The light around me would be golden and gorgeous and redolent of my grief and wronged status. Finally, when I had wept myself out, I would emerge. Now I wanted to do the same. Instead I said, "Yes, I'm upset.

I haven't seen you, I had a horrible, hard week, it's Thanksgiving, and the first thing you do is scold me about the bird shit. It doesn't seem that important."

We were standing in the kitchen regarding each other with dismay, everyone around us trying not to watch.

"I *know*, Meg." She had never been able to take it when I criticized her. "But the bird shit is *really* not good for the car." Inside me, some last plank of steadiness broke. There was nothing motherly about her. The mother in her would have noticed my desperation; she would have put her hands on my shoulders and said *I'm sorry you feel this way, honey, I'm sorry.* This was not my mother. This was a shuffling alien with scary hair.

"Mom, I'm having a hard time."

"I understand that," she said. "But—"

It was too much for me. I erupted. "Mom, you have never supported my divorce, you don't know what this is like—"

"You need to calm down, Meg," she said.

"I do *not* need to calm down," I said. "You are always telling me to calm down. You are always telling me how things are. This is how *I* feel." I dug my fingernails into my arm so deeply they tore the skin open. I pushed up my sleeve and saw blood on my arm. "Do you see what I've done to myself?" I said, in shock. (I was not exactly doing a good job of demonstrating that I didn't need to calm down.) My father on the couch opened his eyes and then closed them, as if he were just too sick to deal with whatever was happening now.

"I'm sorry you feel this way, but it's not true," she continued. "You need to relax."

72

"Look what I've done!" I cried.

Fumbling through tears, I ran upstairs, no longer able to keep up the pretense of being the helpful daughter. I was furious at her confusion, furious at her helplessness. Why was she letting this disease attack her brain? Why was she betraying us? Why was she so mad at *me*?

I went to the bathroom to wash my face and the face that looked back was not my own. I slid down the side of the sink, the cabinet knobs digging into my back, and wept convulsively, clutching my right arm with my left, digging my nails further into the skin of the inner arm, nearer the veins. I felt unsafe, unloved, in pain that could not be borne. I eyed the window. It was too small to escape through.

Desperate, I called my ex-husband, who was at his parents' home, forty minutes away, and, listening to me sob—I couldn't get a word out—he said, "I'm coming to get you." I said, finally, "No, just call me a taxi. I want to leave now."

Liam and Eamon knocked on the door. They told me to stay. "We'll take you to Brooklyn later," Liam said. "You're really upset, and it's not a good idea for you to be alone." They were clearly worried I might hurt myself. But I was not going to hurt myself. I just wanted to flee the pain that lay like a fog in the house; getting away would be like turning a blank page, to a new story, a different one.

Eamon, who has always had a precocious calm in the face of confrontation, hugged me and said, "Of course Mom loves you, she only says wonderful things about you."

"OK," I wailed.

Then our mother was hanging shyly at the door. She seemed uncertain of her role. "Meg," she said, urgency in her voice. "Come in," Eamon said, reaching his arm out to her. Her face crumpled. Suddenly I could see it—the trace hieroglyphics that say *Mother*.

"I don't want anyone to be sad," she said, running her hands through her hair.

"But we are sad, Mom," I said.

"But I don't want you to be."

"It's OK, it's OK for us to be sad, it's natural."

"You're amazing. You are my children. I love you," she said haltingly. "I know you've had a hard time and maybe I have been judgmental. And you're right, it's your feelings, you are the ones who have them. . . . I just don't like to fail you."

Liam said, slowly, "It's OK, Mom. We are going to be sad. It would be weird if we weren't. You have to let us be sad."

"I know," she said at last, crying, nodding. His words always calmed her. "It's just so hard. I just want everyone to be OK. Tell me you'll be OK."

We were in a circle now, hugging. Eamon was slouched over, wiping tears away and looking away, and I was, at once, in ruinous joy and pain, and somehow it was all mixed together like paint, like old stains and water cracks and new color.

Later, Diana told me that when I ran upstairs after my mother and I fought in the kitchen, her ten-year-old son came over and tugged on her sleeve and said, "*What* did Meghan get on the car?" As if learning it could help him understand, as if he could file the information away for safekeeping. Note to self: Do not do *that*.

S HORTLY BEFORE THE HOLIDAY, Jim and I had started talking again. For months we'd been largely estranged, but he was close to my mother and wanted to see her and to help us, and there was something comforting about his familiar presence. That night he came for Thanksgiving dinner, just as he had for the past five years. Perhaps my mother's death would be not unlike a divorce, I found myself thinking, wishfully: I would see her less, but now and then be granted a reprieve like this. It would be a reunion like those in *The Aeneid* or *The Odyssey*, when the heroes go down to the Underworld to see their dead parents and embrace them three times, waking to their disappearance.

I half avoided him on Thanksgiving, but I was glad he was there.

The day after Thanksgiving, I took my mother to the mall. We'd all been milling around reading the *Times*, and I turned to her and said, "Why don't we go shopping? You need some new clothes. You need some pants that you're not holding up with a tape measure."

"Well, I don't want to inconvenience you," she said, then thought for a second. "I *would* like to get some clothes. I could just come with you, as you drop the kids off at the train station. Unless that's an inconvenience," she said again.

"No, it's not." And I realized she was confused—another crack in the foundation—and in her confusion she didn't want to impose on us. She hated being confused. (During this time she would get a look in her eyes that Liam described as "a look of fear, but fear of something she can't name.")

She got us lost on the way to the mall. She thought she knew how to get there from Westport, instead of from the house, but when we were on the highway she blanked on the exit. "I don't know," she said. "I'm sorry, I don't know."

She hit her seat with the flat of her palm. "I am just so damn out of it all the time. I know something is wrong with my brain because I can't remember things."

"It's OK," I said. "You're going to have the radiation in a few days; it's going to help. They said it would help reduce the confusion, and you'll be just like normal."

"I know," she said, "it's just frustrating."

Of course it was. I was stunned by the way my mother's body was being taken to pieces, how each new week brought a new failure, how surreal the disintegration of a body was.

Then she said, without any trace of irony, "I am worried about your father. He's so sick. I just have to get better so I can help him. If I weren't so confused, I could help him feel better. He needs to rest."

. . .

Inside the department store, I fingered a blue silk shirt. "This is nice," I said.

"Yeah," she said. "But I think I have to go to the plus sizes section."

I looked at her.

"Mom, I do not think you have to go to the plus sizes section."

"But that's usually where I shop."

"I know, but it's not now. Trust me."

"Well, OK." And she brightened up.

And I realized: We hadn't shopped together for clothes for fifteen years or so. She felt self-conscious about her weight and so she never bought clothes with anyone; instead, she usually ordered them online, minimizing having to try things on. We started picking pants out for her; she told me to pull out the largest size.

"I don't think so," I said. "I think you are going to be a size twelve."

"No, get me the biggest size."

"OK," I said.

I picked up a soft purple cowl-necked cashmere sweater from the sale table and found some more shirts. When I came back, I heard my mother fumbling.

"Meg? I think these are too big."

I went in. The pants were baggy around her. "Yes, they are. We need to find you a size twelve."

I fingered a pink dress with a paisley print hanging by the dressing room, and my mother, sounding like her usual self, called out, "That's pretty, try that on!"

"I don't need any more dresses."

"Come on, try it on," she said. "It's on sale. You can just come in the dressing room with me," she said, and I did, and we took off our clothes and dressed, and I helped her buckle and snap shirts and pants. She had folds of skin around her stomach but her legs looked tiny, emaciated, like an old person's. She put on the purple cowl-neck sweater with a pair of black dress slacks and looked beautiful, her hair dark, her cheeks flushed.

(It hurts to think about this.)

But her underwear was a disaster. Under the soft sweater, I could see her bra drooping around her sides, hanging loosely, the cup fronts folding and creating a funny extra shelf of flesh.

"Mom," I said, "you need new bras."

"I know," she said, "these are too big, I guess."

"If we are buying you new clothes, we're buying new underwear. We'll do a whole makeover."

She'd been watching a TV show about learning to dress stylishly and she smiled with delight.

"They keep saying you should divide your body in thirds," she said. "And they tell you to get nice fabric and watch the fit. It's interesting. Things about clothes I never would have noticed, I notice now. Like this isn't really fitting right, here. And this fabric feels cheap."

Wearing the cowl-neck, she looked kind of like a sexpot. But a sexpot with a lumpy, saggy bra. I ran upstairs and grabbed an armful of bras in a variety of sizes. I have *no* idea what size I am, my mom had said. And neither did I.

"Can I help you?" said the saleslady.

"Um . . . not really," I said, not knowing how to explain that I was looking for new bras for my dying mother, who'd lost so much weight we had no idea where to begin. I pulled a whole range of styles, including some lace ones—if she was going to die soon, she should at least get to feel sexy and pretty first—and downstairs my mother tried them on. The lace ones, the prettiest, were the wrong size, and she was clearly disappointed. "I'll just get this one," she said, holding up a practical cotton piece. "No, I'm going to get you some more," I said.

"But they're all the way on the other floor," she said, but then she looked at a periwinkle lace bra I had tried on, and said, "That's nice, it's like delft," and so I threw on a shirt and ran to find a better size in the lace.

After, we went through all her clothes, the pants and sweaters, deciding what to keep. As we stood in the dressing room, she looked at them in my arms and a shadow crossed her face. "But this is a lot," she said.

"You need it," I said. And the unspoken thing was there: How long would she need it for? Probably not more than a month or two.

Still. I wanted her to have them. And everything was twenty percent off. I reminded her of this. She got giddy and said, "It *is* a good value." And she smoothed the sweater down and said, "I have cleavage!"

As we paid, she was happy, stroking the clothes like a girl. For a moment I thought, this must be what she'd felt when I was a teenager and she could lift my mood by taking me shopping—a slippery pride, tinged with sadness that it couldn't always be like this.

She fingered a tag. "Size twelve," she sighed. "You see, Meggy, there are some good things about having cancer!"

That night, she gave Diana and my father a fashion show, delightedly going up and down the stairs and coming down with a new outfit on.

As we waited for her surgery, my mother and Liam and Eamon and I watched TV. She spent most of each day on the chaise longue section of the couch. Sometimes her fingers absently traced the fabric and kneaded it, as if to touch a body. The dogs sat on either side, like sphinxes. We watched *Lost*.

"That Evangeline Lilly is so annoying," my mother said. "Why can't she *do* something, instead of talking about it? Why does she always make such terrible choices?" For someone with brain tumors, my mother was doing a fine job of keeping up with the plot twists. (As Jim put it: "Even healthy people can't follow *Lost*. Are you sure you want to watch it?")

In between episodes, when I paused the DVD to go get her a Limonata, you could hear the grandfather clock. *Tick,*

tick, tick, tick. My mother is dying, I would think. And she is spending her last hours watching *Lost*. How totally bizarre. For a moment I hated the show for that. But then I thought: *What the hell. What is she supposed to do, contemplate every moment with saintly beatitude? Exclaim that she loves us, is devastated to be leaving us, cannot bear not to watch Eamon graduate from college, to see our children?* Time doesn't obey our commands. You cannot make it holy just because it is disappearing.

Other people—friends, colleagues—got used to my mother dying of cancer. But I did not. Each day, sunlight came like a knife to a wound that was not healed.

CHAPTER FIVE

caretaking

Even though it was obvious by Thanksgiving that my mother was extremely sick, the swiftness of her final days came as a surprise. She'd had CyberKnife radiation in Stamford; it had made her more confused for a while—the surgery caused a supposedly temporary swelling—which meant she couldn't be alone. I'd gone up to Connecticut on Sunday to see her and to talk to my father and brothers about arranging for hospice care. She was getting weaker and we needed to be ready; even if her confusion diminished, as was supposed to happen, she was losing weight and clearly declining. And yet we were all acting as though she were going to be around forever, if in an increasingly diminished state. Working up my courage—there was a way in which we all just wanted to be silent—I said as much to my brothers and Dad and they agreed. "We'll talk about it tomorrow," they said.

The next day, Liam and I took her for a follow-up visit with the neurosurgeon in Stamford. Her confusion had lasted longer than the doctors anticipated. She had a hard time locating the doctor's office—I got lost driving her there and we were fifteen minutes late—and she struggled with finding the correct words when she spoke. She wanted to know if she could drive. This was clearly not possible, but the doctor was rude about it. "No, absolutely not," he said unfeelingly, not acknowledging that this news might be hard for her to hear. Her face flushed and she slumped back in her chair at his words.

I asked whether the confusion she was experiencing was a normal side effect, and he dismissively replied, "We didn't give you any guarantees that this surgery would work."

"I'm not asking for guarantees," I said, enunciating each word. "I'm trying to have a conversation with you that will enable us to understand just a little better what is going on." *Prick.*

My mother stirred and said, "Meg . . ." and I bit my tongue. She was never confrontational with her doctors.

My mother cried on the way home, trying not to let us see. But as we walked into the house, she leaned on us to climb the steps and said, crisply, "That asshole would never have been so patronizing if you weren't so small, Meg." And then she said, "He doesn't know that you're big inside." That night she seemed more herself than in weeks, joking with

Isabel and Diana on the phone. Her locutions were slightly off, but poetically. When Diana asked how she felt, my mother responded, "I hurt less." It was a windy night, and we sat and watched—as it happened—a particularly stormy episode of *Lost*. A gust of wind howled outside. Mom turned and said, "Is that *our* wind I hear?"

Later, as I came out of my room, there she was, leaning on the stair railing, climbing one foot at a time. She paused. She looked more and more striking in those last days. Objectively, I know she was ill: I have photos on my phone that show her sallow and drawn. But not taking chemo meant her skin had some of its old glow. The lost weight made her appear young and slightly transparent. I often had the feeling she was passing into a liminal state.

"Good night, Meggy," she said, playfully, even happily. "I love you to death." She used the voice she used when I was a child—that old good night.

The next morning, she was delirious. Her mouth slack, she was twisted up in the sheets. My father hovered over me. We were trying to wake her. "Mom," I said, shaking her shoulder a bit. She groaned in annoyance. "Mom," I said, and her eyes opened, but they weren't hers. She looked possessed. Instead of fear of what she couldn't name, now there was hatred of all that she had once been close to. Her skin was hot to the touch.

"Did you take her temperature?" I asked.

"No," he said. "She's always hot when she wakes up."

"Not like this," I said. I got the thermometer and tried to get it under her tongue, but she kept pushing it away. By now she was moaning and clutching her right side. When I touched her stomach there it was extremely warm, and the skin was distended.

My dad was pacing. "We have an appointment with the pain specialist," he said, "so if you could just get her dressed."

"I don't think she needs the pain specialist," I said. "I think she needs the emergency room."

"I don't want to go to the emergency room," he said. "Let's just get her to the doctor."

Fine, I said. But I thought: This is not going to work.

She had on only a T-shirt and underwear. "Mom," I said, "we have to get you dressed. We're going to get you dressed and then take you to the doctor."

She kept batting my hand away. Then she said, "I want to go to the bathroom."

I lifted her up and she cried out, seizing her side. I knew that one of the risks of her cancer—which tends to metastasize first to the lungs and the liver—was that the liver would begin to fail. It was, my doctor friend had told me, one of the two things that was most likely to kill her. The other was a hemorrhage in the lungs. I had been assuming the failing liver would be less awful than blood-filled lungs. Now I was questioning that assumption. She collapsed back on the bed and refused to talk to me.

"Call the ER," I told my dad.

. . .

The paramedics came, three of them. In some obscure way I noticed one of them was good-looking. My mother was confused and angry and rolled her eyes at us like we had betrayed her, and it felt like we had. The paramedics kept saying, "Barbara, come on, we're just going to get you on the stretcher." I'd tried to get her pants on before they came, so she wouldn't feel embarrassed, but I hadn't managed to.

"Fine," she finally said, seeming to come to her senses. "But I have to go to the bathroom." They had her by both arms. I shook my head at them. I knew she was just trying to get away. But my father said, "Let's let her go."

"OK, Barbara," they said. They led her into the bathroom and then they said to me, "Do you want to help her from here?" She refused to look at me. She went in and closed the door.

Minutes passed.

"I think we need to get her out," one of the guys said.

"No fucking kidding," I said, full of a weird I-told-you-so anger at everyone.

"Does one of you want to try?" they said.

Did I want to *try*? No, I did not want to try.

My dad went forward. "Kell," he said, using his pet name for her. "Come on, Kell, we have to go. Let me help you."

"Go away."

Come on Kell, I'll help you.

I'd never heard my father's voice like this before. It was his voice for her, intimate, direct, adoring—clearly the voice he'd used when they were alone together, in their tender moments. She refused to answer.

"Meg," he said, coming out, "I can't get her, can you?"

I hate you, I thought.

But I was her daughter.

"Mom," I said. "Come on, we're just going to go to the hospital so they can give you some medicine."

"Go away," she said. "Leave me alone."

She wouldn't look at me. She sat on the toilet, underwear (the underwear we'd just bought) at her ankles.

My book of poems was on the toilet behind her, along with Darwin's *The Origin of Species*, her favorite book. And a crossword she'd started two Sundays ago.

I stepped forward to take her arm.

She batted me away.

"Dad," I said, "we're going to have to pull her out."

So I went in and I grabbed her under her shoulders and I lifted her up and she struggled and I collapsed a little inside and she grabbed for her underwear but couldn't reach it so I pulled it up as my father took her other arm—the room was too small for both of us so he was reaching in awkwardly—and we hoisted her out as she went tense with anger and frustration.

I thought of her when she was happy—her voice the night before when she said, "I love you to death"—and I wondered which was the real her. The other is, I thought. But her anger was so vivid, it was easy to believe this was the unmasked truth: She was dying, and she hated us.

She didn't stay in the hospital for long: they released her, because she wouldn't drink barium for a CAT scan. I'd had to drive into New York for a business dinner, and my father was alone with her. He called me to say they were sending her home because her fever had gone down, and since she wouldn't drink the barium they had "no reason for admitting her." They can't send her home, I said. What about the fact that she has terminal cancer? Is that not a reason? I'd just finished talking to the hospice people and they'd told me it would be forty-eight hours before they could get someone to us. "We're not set up to take care of her," I told my father, but he said, in a thick voice, "She wants to go home, I have to do what she wants," and hung up on me. I slammed my phone shut. (At the time, I was so bent on her safety—or at least my idea of her safety—that I wanted to kill him; now it is much easier for me to understand why he had to take her home.) I'd planned to stay in Brooklyn but was too disturbed to do so; I drove back up to my parents' house and fell into bed. Thirty minutes later, there was a horrible crash in the other room and I heard my mother screaming. The sound, at once piercing and soft, was like nothing I'd ever heard, and for a couple of minutes I couldn't get out of bed. Then doors were opening. In my parents' room, my mom was on the floor, crying, holding her head and her side, and Liam and my dad were standing, and Eamon was cradling her head, kneeling over, saying, "Where does it hurt? Shhh, it's OK, where does it hurt, Mom?" Liam knelt next to her and was stroking her arm.

"Let's try to get her up," Dad said.

"Let's just wait and see if she starts to feel better in a few minutes," Eamon said, patting her head.

"I think we should call the ER," I said, pacing. "I don't think this is getting better. I think something is really wrong."

"Then call the fucking ER," someone snapped.

I felt my inky heart spilling open everywhere. How could my father have allowed this to happen? I went down and called 911. The operator said the paramedics would be there in twenty minutes. And they were and so it began all over— the maneuvering of her body, the gurney, the screaming, the rolling of eyes. I got in my car and Eamon came with me. Liam went in the ambulance and my dad drove his car. We drove through the pouring rain; at the hospital—it was a different hospital this time—we were all bleary-eyed; it was extremely bright. The orderly on duty said only two of us could go back into the ER with her.

"Look," I said to him, "what's your name?"

He told me.

"Look, you can understand, maybe—our mother has terminal cancer, and we don't know what's going on. We're really worried about her. If it's quiet back there, can we all be with her? We want to be with her together, in case . . ." I let the thought dangle.

"What kind of cancer does she have?"

"Colorectal," I said.

"Oh, that's tough," he said. "My mother died last year from that, it was rough, man. Yeah, OK, but I may need you to not all be there later."

"OK," I said. "We'll do whatever if you just help us out when you can."

At three a.m., the nurses got her settled and sedated and stabilized, and we finally left. Eamon and I drove back together. I was wondering if she'd still be alive in the morning. If she started to die, would the nurses know? Could they call us? How long would dying take, anyway? Eamon put in *Pet Sounds*, and as I drove slowly through the fog and pouring rain we sang along to "Sloop John B," belting out, *"Well, I feel so broke up, I want to go home."*

EXHAUSTED, we took shifts. My dad went in the morning, then came home to take Liam and Eamon to lunch. Isabel was there when I arrived. Her eyes were blurred with tears and sorrow. But she and my mother had actually had a real conversation.

"I got in the bed with her," Isabel said. "She told me how much she loved me. She asked me to crawl into bed with her. She was funny, and clear. We lay together there, like sisters," she said, wiping her eyes. I was cravenly envious. All night I'd dreamed that my mother had died hating us and wondered if I had become the emblem of what was killing her: the daughter taking over the mother's life. Off you go, Mom! Off to the hospital! I'll take over now! But I knew I should be happy for Isabel. And maybe my mother was back.

I went in.

"Hi, Mom," I said.

She looked at me indifferently. As I stood there, the nurse brought her a child-size ice cream cup. "Here," I said, "I'll give you some." And I opened it and pulled off the tiny wooden spoon and offered her a bite. She took one, her mouth opening like a child's; inside, her tongue and cheeks were coated with a white film. I wiped my eyes, holding the ice cream awkwardly.

"Sweetie, I can do that," Isabel said, leaning forward. "Give me the ice cream."

I clutched it to my chest. "It's OK, I want to feed her," I said.

My mother was eyeing us. Scoldingly she told me, "Let Bel do it if she wants to."

A bolt of shame and anger went through me, as it does when you're a child. My mother was dying and she had not, for one moment in the last twenty-four hours, acted like my mother; she'd acted like someone who disliked me. In all my various imaginings of the awful end I knew was to come, I had never pictured an estrangement such as this. Handing Isabel the ice cream, I left the room in tears and went outside to the parking lot, where I leaned against a chill concrete wall and wept. Then I wiped my face and went back inside. I was still here and so was she.

. . .

Those were strange, delirious days. They'd give her morphine for the pain, but the moment they got it under control, it would intensify, and she'd begin moaning again. When she did wake, she was irritable. We made a point of all crowding into the room at one point, and Eamon was trying, in his brave way, to joke with her, and she said something like "That's not funny" (could this really be what she said?) and I watched his face fall. I kept asking the nurses to give her more morphine.

"OK," the nurse said, "but she might just drift away." And then she said: "You have to decide what kind of care you want her on. If she's in hospice, they'll give her more drugs, they'll minimize her pain, but she might die."

I was all for more medicine, more comfort. My brothers and father were not. "What if she gets better?" they kept saying.

Eamon said, "She's confused because of the drugs, we shouldn't give her more."

"It's not because of the drugs that she's confused," I said, insistent, rigid in my certainty. "It's because of her liver."

My father wiped tears from his eyes. "I guess you're right," he said. "But let's just think about it. We don't have to decide right now."

Alone in the room with her while she was sleeping, I slowly pulled her shirt up and looked at her liver, or what they kept saying was her liver, somewhere under the skin. The belly was distended. I put my hand on it lightly but was too nervous to press—though for some reason I needed to feel it, the liver that was failing, hard as stone.

The strangest thing was that the whole time she was impeccably polite and charming to the nurses. I was proud of her but also jealous of the attention she gave them. As soon as a nurse walked into the room she opened her eyes and smiled. Late Thursday, they moved her to the cancer floor, wheeling her bed through the hallways as we trotted to keep up. She had a suite with a pullout couch and a potted plastic plant and a Zenith TV that looked like it was from 1962. She went straight to sleep; Liam stayed with her, and the rest of us went home to sleep.

The next morning, Liam called. "Mom is better," he said.

I could hear relief in his voice. "She's eating some food, and she's totally clearheaded."

Thank God we hadn't medicated her to death. I got there as soon as I could, using the proper entrance instead of the shabby ER doors, and took the elevator up to my mother's room. She was sitting up, a plate of eggs and pancakes on her tray, and Liam was next to her, on the phone. She waved. Her eyes were bright. Part of me still didn't trust her.

"I've been enjoying some pancakes," she said. (She'd had about three bites, by the looks of it.) Then she laughed. "Did

Liam tell you what I did? I was reading the hospital menu, trying to order, and I guess there are all these special menus—the low cholesterol menu, the heart-healthy menu, and when I opened it I went straight to the 'Deathbed Menu.' And I thought: *That's grim!*" Tears of laughter ran down her cheeks. "I didn't have my glasses on. It's really a *diabetic* menu."

Her fever had broken. The doctors conjectured that two things had caused her delirium. The doctors who had done the radiation surgery had put her on too high a dose of steroids, causing not just "irritability" (a common side effect of steroids) but actual delusion and dementia. At the same time, she had a urinary tract infection, which was exacerbating everything, and the first hospital had missed it. What the doctors also said, when I pressed them in the hall outside her room, was that her liver was probably experiencing "necrosis." There's no ammonia building up in her brain, they said, but soon there probably will be.

While Liam and my dad went to work, I tried to organize her release from the hospital. "I just want to go home," she kept saying. We'd arranged for hospice, and all that was needed was for the hospital to approve her discharge. But they wouldn't do it until there was a hospital bed at home, and the insurance company was dragging its feet.

"I have to warn you," the head nurse said, standing in the doorway of my mother's suite, "I don't think this is going to happen today, which means it won't happen till Monday, because the insurance companies are closed over the weekend."

"They're *closed*?" I hissed. If the deli could be open

twenty-four hours, surely an insurance approval line could be, I thought. And I was struck by how much control over these most intimate decisions—decisions about when and where and how my mother would die—we'd given to doctors and insurance companies. I knew, of course, why this had happened, why I had put my mother in circumstances she desperately disliked. Morphine, painkillers: these are good things. When she first went back into the hospital, I had felt reassured: She was getting fluids! She was hydrated again. She would be OK. But it pained me to think that she would have to spend extra days, precious days, in the hospital because *we could not get permission to bring her home*. Whose death was this, after all?

"Meg?" my mother called from the bathroom. "I just fell." I went in and lifted her up. She needed someone to lift her from the toilet each time she used it now; Liam had warned me. I was already getting used to doing it. It made sense. It was what she had done for us, back before we became private and civilized about our bodies. In some ways I liked it. A level of anxiety about the body had been stripped away, and we were left with the simple reality: Here it was.

I heard a lot about the idea of dying "with dignity" while my mother was sick. It was only near her very end that I gave much thought to what this idea meant. I didn't actually feel it was undignified for my mother's body to fail—that was the human condition. Having to help my mother on and off the toilet was difficult, but it was natural. The real indignity, it seemed, was dying where no one cared for you the way your family did, dying where it was hard for your whole family to be with you and where excessive measures might be taken to keep you alive past a moment that called for letting go. I didn't want that for my mother. I wanted her to be able to go home. I didn't want to pretend she wasn't going to die.

Eamon stayed with her that night. When I came the next day to spell him, she told me what a nice time they'd had. "He just needed to see me," she said. "He needed to watch a movie and talk." Our mother! Here she was. Surely she would never leave us again; we needed her.

"I think Eamon's hitting it off with the nurse," she continued. "She comes in a lot more when he's visiting."

"Which one?" I said, hitting the morphine button to give her a boost, which made me feel I wasn't useless.

"Christine—Nicole—I can't remember. They all have names like Christine or Nicole."

My father called that afternoon to say that he and Eamon had the stomach flu and were throwing up. He wanted to know if I could stay another night.

My mother needed to see a local oncologist before the hospital would let her go home: more emergencies might occur, and she wouldn't be going to New York anymore to see Mears. It was a Saturday, and the only oncologist around was a doctor named Malefatto. After a silent double take—his name, traced to Italian roots, sounded a lot like Dr. "Wrongdoing" or Dr. "Badly Done"—I asked the nurse to send him to our room when he did rounds.

Dr. Badly Done turned out to be kind. And he did well

something that is easily done badly: he told my mother she had a few days or weeks left to live, a fact she had not quite taken in. It was his job to tell her that she had to decide whether she wanted to become a "hospice patient"—to receive only pain management rather than major interventions. He said something about "what remained to be done"; my mother misunderstood him and said she didn't want any chemotherapy. He corrected her: "There's really no more chemotherapy we can do," he said. In that moment, I saw my mother realize, anew, what she had realized earlier that fall when Mears had told her there were no remaining treatments.

"So," she said slowly, "there is nothing left to do?"

"No," said Dr. Malefatto.

My mother's face grew still. I could see how strange this was to her, as it was to me. Five days earlier, she'd been walking around, even going to work for an hour here and there. Now she couldn't stand without one of us lifting her. How had we gotten here so fast? Then she looked at me.

"I have to call your father and tell him," she said. I didn't say: He already knows.

Things My Mother Said:

To my father: "All right, I'll go to bed, but only if I can walk backward."

To all of us: "I'd really like to get into a nice pair of terjamas."

To the three-year-old daughter of a friend at her school: "I have a boo-boo, too."

ONE OF THE IDEAS I've clung to most of my life is that if I just try hard enough it will work out. If I work hard, I will be spared, and I will get what I desire, finding the cave opening over and over again, thieving life from the abyss. This sturdy belief system has a sidecar in which superstition rides. Until recently, I half believed that if a certain song came on the radio just as I thought of it, it meant that all would be well. What did I mean? I preferred not to answer that question. To look too closely was to prick the balloon of possibility. I also held the delusion that the imperfect could be fixed by attention. And so in the hospital I was always eager to show the nurses what I knew, how much I had learned, including the fact that I had to prostrate myself before their wisdom, experience, and sore feet. I was the model relative, slipping out along the linoleum hallway in my thick stay-over socks, delicately catching the attention of the receptionist and saying, "I see that my mother's morphine is about to run out. I wonder if someone could change it before it starts beeping and wakes her—I know," leaning in confidingly, like a student bowing her head to a good teacher, "that we need to stay *ahead* of the pain." I would pause a beat. "I know you're all so busy, I just don't want my mother"—a slight stress on the word, another pause, almost imperceptible, so that the nurse could think *my mother my mother* and remember her own mother, who perhaps had cradled her and nursed her, the only relationship like that we have, mysterious, impenetrable, luxurious—

"to suffer." And I'd exhale. And the strapped receptionist wouldn't smile, but she would say, "I'll try to signal the floor nurse for you, honey."

Doctors and nurses are the family members' priests: we supplicate them, please let us go, just let us go home, we recite their catechism, we assure them we will not blame them, we just want her to be at home, we will not sue you. These nurses were our benefactors. They were the ones who did all the work. The doctors knew things but Had to Get On. The nurses administered the morphine. They adjusted the bed. They washed my mother and helped her take a shower. They were a sorority, eager, optimistic, burned-out. I liked the receptionist. She was tough, and she saw through my wheedling show, but she helped me anyway, because she understood that underneath the performance lay not manipulation but desperation. In these moments, sliding back to my mother's room, past the room of another woman dying of cancer whose daughter, about my age, much taller, elegant and thin, showed up regularly with her two young children, and irregularly with her husband, and who caused, in me, a flicker of envy, of what-might-have-been, a whiff of the perennial outsider, so that even here, even now, where I knew we were facing the Real Deal, where I was being changed, altered, every day by it, I would experience the exact same twinge I used to feel in eighth grade at the sight of a peer who was put together and clean-limbed in all the ways I never felt, and here she was, yet again, taunting me with her family, her two ten-fingered and ten-toed children, as she, like me, bent, adjusted pillows, brought flowers, cajoled nurses. *Your grief is not like mine,* I thought spitefully. *You're going home to your family. I am newly divorced. I have no family. All I have is this: I have devoted myself to understanding death so that afterward I can say that I was there, fully there.* And in this perverse manner I somehow believed, and still do, sitting here with my books and my words, using my mind to scavenge every last scrap of meaning from the bones of these old ways, that I could lift the window in that dim, grimy Bridgeport hospital room and take my mother's bony hand and slip out, out into the street, past the hospital awning into the royal purple evening and then out into the sea, the dark green sea.

And then the noises would return. I could hear the coughing man whose family talked about sports and sitcoms every time they visited, sitting politely around his bed as if you couldn't see the death knobs that were his knees poking through the blanket, but as they left they would hug him and say, We love you, and We'll be back soon, and in their voices and in mine and in the nurse who was so gentle with my mother, tucking cool white sheets over her with a twist of her wrist, I could hear love, love that sounded like a rope, and I began to see a flickering electric current everywhere I looked as I went up and down the halls, flagging nurses, little flecks of light dotting the air in sinewy lines, and I leaned on these lines like guy ropes when I was so tired I couldn't walk anymore and a voice in my head said: *Do you see this love? And do you still not believe?*

I couldn't deny the voice.

Now I think: That was exhaustion.

But at the time the love, the love, it was like ropes around me, cables that could carry us up into the higher floors away from our predicament and out onto the roof and across the empty spaces above the hospital to the sky where we could gaze down upon all the people driving, eating, having sex, watching TV, angry people, tired people, happy people, all doing, all being—

Of course this didn't happen; I got the nurse, and she replaced the morphine bag. And then my mother shuffled over to the couch with her IV pole and we curled up, and I pulled out my laptop and scooted close to her and we watched an episode of some show on DVD. Periodically the computer would freeze and we'd shake it.

I tried to sleep on the pullout couch but its plastic mattress was noisy. I made the couch back up and sat on it. Machines beeped all around me in the antiseptic hallways. Every now and then my mother moaned. I got up to give her a jolt of morphine. Outside the window lay Bridgeport Harbor, one of the least picturesque pieces of waterfront on the northeast seaboard. The city lights were a peculiar wan orange. The room in which my mother lay was functional, scattered with coyly folding plastic tables, buttons for reclining and inclining, and wee tubes of toothpaste. (You won't be needing much.) This is where we die, I thought, stripped of any fleck of the festive. Dying is bureaucratic and fluorescent. Beyond the window, a Metro-North train pulled into the station and paused. The timing was so familiar from my trips on the train to see my parents that I imagined I could hear the ding signaling the doors were about to close, and the gravelly voice announcing this was the train to New Haven. I turned the words over in my mind. I could see the small outlines of figures within, like characters in a story, a Cheever story perhaps, going home to their unhappy, flawed homes, the only homes we have on this planet, the train swinging smoothly along the tracks, lit up and shiny, silhouettes bending over their magazines and computers, pressing onward into the night.

In the morning, when she woke, she said to me, "Can you take me home, honey? I think if I go home I'll feel better. I'll be able to straighten my throat." She gestured to her throat. "It needs to uncrinkle. Last night I dreamed that you were all in the living room with me at home, and you all were sitting in the chairs very straight, and I couldn't do it, and I was very frustrated. And you told me if I just moved chairs I'd be able to sit straight like the rest of you, and I wanted to, but I couldn't get out of my chair."

I GOT THE FLU my father and Eamon had. Driving back from the hospital, I developed a heavy feeling in my stomach. I went to bed early. I woke nauseated an hour later and vomited up my dinner in the toilet.

I was so sick I couldn't sleep. I threw up again and again, unable to keep water down or get as far as the bathroom. For some reason—I can't remember why, exactly, except that we were so clearly in need of help—Jim was there, and he cleaned everything up. "You don't have to do that," I said weakly.

"It's OK," he said matter-of-factly, wiping my vomit from the floor with an old towel. The dog came in, wagging his tail, then Eamon behind him.

Eamon knelt by my bed, almost still a child, growing into himself. "Hey Meg," he said softly. "Hey, I think you should smoke some of this. It'll make you feel better." He pulled a joint out of his pocket and held it up hopefully.

"It helped me when I was so sick," he said. "I gave some to Mom and it helped her."

"OK," I said.

He took out his kelly-green lighter and lit it, and took a hit, the end blazing orange as a firefly. Then he handed it to me and I did, too.

Maybe I could get so stoned the hospital would recede to a tiny box, and when I returned, I'd feel like Gulliver, or a psychedelically tall Alice, able to peer down at the minuscule efforts of the medics, and think, Far out, far, far out, before returning slowly to my real life.

Then we fought, my father and I; it was snowing, my mother was in the hospital, I came home, I was tired, I had to teach, I took my mother's car. You can't take that, said my father, and I told him I wasn't a child anymore. When people are hurting they cannot always comfort one another; it was true of us. We had the same injury and different symptoms. We were on the landing; my brothers emerged from their rooms to calm us down, but we couldn't be calmed. If I'm going to help you I have to be helped in return, I said to my father, I need to borrow the car. Don't blackmail me, he said, I can't believe you would blackmail me at a time like this. Of course I was not blackmailing him but he was the bleeding front of a war, a war that was going badly, and all its resources were here, bleeding out, being badly used. I'll worry about you, and I can't have that, he said. You don't get to decide that, I said, and thought, *You don't get to decide, not just because I'm thirty-two years old, but because to live is to worry, to wonder when the last hour comes, as it one day will.* I thought of us fishing together in the past that was now always past except when we remembered it, him showing me how to thread the line, all the hours still to be used before both of us, the sun shining more shimmeringly in memory than it ever could now. But I was bereft and that made me cold and I had no sympathy for him, I was just alight with anger.

Now I think it was cowardly of me—so cowardly—not to have paused to imagine how terrified he was. But to get through the awful days I had to be persuaded of the absolute reality of the tunnel I crawled through. Otherwise I might have merely fallen to the ground in despair.

The insurance company was dragging its feet about the hospital bed. And so she couldn't leave on Friday. On Sunday I went back to Brooklyn, exhausted, to get clothes and do some work. My father and brothers got her home on Monday.

She called me. "I'm home, Meg!" she said.

A flush of happiness spread through me. She was safe. Safe with a hospital bed. A funny kind of safe, but I was glad.

By the next day, when I got back, the confusion had begun to return. Right. Her death was still going to happen.

CHAPTER SIX

the end

The hospital bed has been set up in the living room, and now she divides her days between the couch in the den and the bed in the living room, a bright, open room painted a pale blue, with a picture window looking onto the lawn and the pond and a tall stand of pines. (I want to be near things that are much older than I am, she'd told me in the hospital, things that will be here after I'm gone.) We have put up Christmas decorations and they hang slightly lopsided around us, the lights sparkling on the porch as usual. But we all know that for us there will never be an as usual again.

As she sits on the couch, I bring her yogurt and rub her feet with lavender lotion. She sighs. It is the only thing I can do that brings her pleasure.

I keep counting minutes under my breath, telling myself, *She is still here.*

Every morning the hospice nurse comes for two hours. Each visit starts the same way: On a scale of one to ten, Barbara, with one being the lowest and ten being the highest, how bad is your pain? They say it fast and singsong, like a prayer or a sales pitch. My mother takes to holding up her fingers, not bothering to speak: seven fingers. Soon we need the walker. Then we need the toilet adjuster, because we can't lift her off the seat. Then we need the diapers. I am glad that we have hospice. But as Liam puts it, "My friends keep saying how great it is that we have hospice. And I want to say, Have you done it? It's not exactly a cozy picnic. The word sounds so nice, like hospitality, but the reality is awful." Yet it is far better than the alternative, we know.

One day I wake in a bad mood. Melancholy: the black sorrow, bilious, angry, a slick in my chest.

I have a question today for those who run the universe: *She tried hard. She did her best. She didn't complain. She took all the fucking medicine. We helped her. We put the poisons down her throat, then cooked bland food for her. Don't we get something for that?*

For that, we get a social worker.

"Hi there, are you" (looking at her paperwork) "Meghan?" she asks brightly, standing on our doorstep.

"Yes," I say. I am sullen already. I have made a mistake. I have told the hospice people—the nice, bright, clear hospice people—that we want a social worker. Now I realize: *We so,*

so, so do not want a social worker. I know it already. Her de-
meanor informs me. They told me a social worker could help
us figure out how to get my mother in and out of bed. Instead, she wants to make us feel better. I don't want to feel
better. She is also, I decide immediately and cruelly, dumb.
Unfortunately, we *are* having trouble getting Mom in and out
of bed. And we need help.

"Here," I'd said yesterday morning to my mother. "Put
your arms around me."

She put her arms around me. "OK."

I lifted. We got her twenty-five degrees up off the couch
and then I couldn't lift anymore. I was too short. She fell
back down and grunted. *Uoph.*

That didn't work.

She was making a face, the pain face.

Liam came to help. He's taller and much stronger.

"Put your arms around me," he said.

She put her arms around his neck.

The walker was getting all tangled up in his legs.

"OK, here we go." He lifted. He had a better angle.

She was up, sort of. "Let me go," she said irritably to me
when I took her arm. "Give me the walker."

She got the walker. She pushed it across the floor. She
went into the bathroom. Silence. We waited.

Do we go stand outside the door?

Should we be listening to our mother urinate?

Should we be letting her stand and sit on her own?
Should we be letting her fall, as she does, when we let her go
in alone?

. . .

The social worker introduces herself to my dad. Eamon walks into the kitchen and pulls me over. "Who's that?" he says. He's already bristling. "Why is she here? Too many people have been here," he says. "They're bothering Mom."

"She's the social worker," I say. "I called her. She's supposed to help us." He rolls his eyes. She comes out of the bathroom and I answer some basic questions.

"Now I'd like to ask your mom some questions," she says, with a faux-cheery voice.

"You can try," I say. My mother has been mostly unconscious for the past twelve hours.

We go into the room and sit by the hospital bed. Ringo, lying at the foot of the bed, stiffens and growls when the woman enters, which I have never seen him do; Eamon hovers, protectively.

"Barbara?" the woman says. "Hi, I'm here to help you and your family out. I just want to ask you some questions." My mother opens her eyes and gives the social worker the Skeleton Face. For some reason, she is alert and focused—as if sensing intrusion.

The social worker begins her questioning. "When were you first diagnosed?" she asks. She has just asked me these questions.

"May of 2006," Mom says.

"And did you take chemotherapy?"

"Yes."

"And when did you stop the chemotherapy?"

"September," my mother says wearily, looking at the ceiling.

"And then you were in the hospital just now?"

"Yes."

"And how have you been doing since you were in the hospital? Are you getting everything you need?"

My mother slowly looks around the room. I have answered all these questions. The social worker was supposed to show us how to take care of my mother, not torment her with details. But she is one of those people who is enamored of her own slight power over the distraught and diseased.

"Have you seen or would you like to see a priest or a minister?" the woman asks.

At this, my mother rouses herself, fixes her eyes on the woman, and asks, "What exactly is the point of these questions?"

"I just—we just want to figure out where you're coming from," the social worker stutters, taken aback.

"I know exactly where I came from," my mother says slowly, as if she is speaking to a moron. "I'm much more interested in where I'm *going*."

Eamon and I can't help it. We start giggling.

Still, she does show us how to lift my mother. The key, it turns out, is getting her firmly from under the shoulders.

EVERY TIME my mother goes to the bathroom with her walker it makes a scratching sound against the kitchen's stone floor. *Scritch-scratch. Scritch-scratch.* Her eyes have begun to go vacant. Her hair is a mess. Soon my mother can no longer stand, and then she is half asleep all the time. The hospice nurse comes one day and says, I think we need to let her just lie here. She washes her with a warm cloth. We take turns sleeping on the couch. When it is my turn, I wake up in the middle of the night and see that my father has come downstairs and is standing in his sweatshirt looking at her in the darkness, fists punched into his sweatshirt pouch, shoulders hunched. He stands for minutes, gazing down on her sleeping face.

Isabel and Diana come to sit with her and say their goodbyes. For some reason this, more than anything, makes her impending death real to me. I can't look in their teary faces.

My father brings home a Christmas tree and puts lights on it and decorates it. It's five feet from my mother's bed, and the warm glow of the colored lights on her face makes her look tan. The pine smell is sharp. Lying there, reading one night, I keep thinking of a Basho haiku:

> Even in Kyoto—
> Hearing the cuckoo's cry—
> I long for Kyoto.

Sometimes I just sit on the couch with a quilt and a book and read beside her. I want to be next to her as much as I can. I have found an old copy of *The Hound of the Baskervilles* in the basement rec room, the copy she gave me for Christmas when I was in fourth grade, and I read it early in the morning next to her, remembering myself as a child getting up early, reading on the sleeping bag, her sleeping in the room next door and eventually waking and saying, "Hi, Meg."

She moans in her sleep. I press the pump to give her the bolus, the extra shot of morphine you could give every thirteen minutes.

I love and hate the bolus. Am I even referring to it properly? I don't know; I never quite learn the name. And why can't she just have the bolus all the time? Why must she be in pain? Click. There's another shot. Sometimes I get impatient and click it before it's ready. And it beeps hostilely at me. *Beep*.

Eamon hates the bolus. He hates the Ativan. He thinks the drugs are making her confused. "Let's just try giving her less drugs," he keeps saying, but I can't stand my mother's pain.

S LEEPING beside my mother's body again, as I did many years ago, I have only grown hungry for more of her. For suddenly the mother is everywhere. She is in the room: expansive, calm, the same brow and mouth. I wake up in the night, hear her breathing—long suck in, two short sucks out; long suck in, two short sucks out, the space between them getting longer and longer—think, *She'll be dead in three days, easy,* and suddenly can't breathe. I reach for her Ativan and take one. Otherwise I don't sleep at all.

Then she cries in her sleep and her face twists and there's that weird demon again, and I look away. I wonder: If I believe she will live, if I say *No,* if I refuse—will she not just go on living?

I think: It's the holidays. There are parties. I'm young. I've spent the past two years going to oncologists. I'm going to put on my party shoes. And I do go to one party, and I leave when people start to dance around a pole. Later I start dating the man whose party it was, and he remembers being glad I came, and casually tells me how he flirted his head off that night. I'm not in your country, I think. I haven't lived in your country for a while.

My ex-husband comes to say goodbye. We've all been sick; there's no food in the house. He goes grocery shopping and carries wood in from the porch. My mother has been mostly in what resembles a coma. But as he walks through the foyer, which opens onto the living room, she opens her eyes and says, just like usual, "Hi, Jim!" Then she closes her eyes again.

These are the last words I hear her say. Instead of words there comes a horrible pain—pain of a kind I have never witnessed, a shuddering, bone-deep pain that swallows her up whenever the hospice nurse moves her or washes her or when we roll her on her side to change her and get her blood circulating.

In these last three days, she begins to look very young. Her face has lost so much weight, the bones show through like a child's. Her eyebrows and eyelashes are very black. Not sort of black. Very black. I hold her hand. I smooth her face. Her skin has begun to feel waxy; my fingers slide dully over it. Also there are little grains all over her face, as if she is in the midst of exfoliating.

As she dies, two hours after we open our presents, in a charade of our usual holiday, she opens her eyes, looks at us, and takes one final rattling breath. She has not opened her eyes for days. How can she not be full of intention? She has chosen to look at us, to say *Goodbye, I love you, goodbye*.

Later, Liam gamely jokes that she died because I said I was going for a run. As soon as I did, her breathing slowed. "She didn't want to wait that long," Liam says. He shoots me a look. "And she knew you'd be pissed if we were all here and you weren't." And his voice breaks.

Our mother was a fierce driver. A leased BMW was her one luxury—she didn't have fancy clothes or jewelry, other than a few necklaces and earrings my dad gave her, and a ring from Isabel. She was protective of the car and proud of it. "I love driving it!" she would say, almost purring. The summer before she died, Jim came up to Connecticut with me for dinner; he'd just bought a used Audi. "Barbara," he said, "I have to show you something." My mother had just begun her final round of chemotherapy, but she disentangled the chemo purse from her chair and walked haltingly out to the driveway. When she saw the car, she cried out in glee, looked at Jim, and said, "We should race!"

It was always apparent that she was alive, Eamon says as we talk about her in his room. There was a calm vibrancy to her. She was essentially impossible to knock off her balance. But she wasn't stagnant. She was always moving. She had found the equilibrium.

While we talk, he lies on the bed, his arms stretched overhead, a woolen ski cap with ear flaps perched precariously on his head, as if he needed protection from the cold. The room is strewn with clothes.

I think she had the most beautiful smile in the world, he says. And she was very warm to lie next to, soft, like a blanket.

II

CHAPTER SEVEN

yearning

In the weeks after my mother's death, I experienced an acute
nostalgia. This longing for a lost time was so intense I thought
it might split me in two, like a tree hit by lightning. I was—as
the expression goes—flooded by memories. It was a submer-
sion in the past that threatened to overwhelm any "rational"
experience of the present, water coming up around my
branches, rising higher. I did not care much about work I
had to do. I was consumed by memories of seemingly trivial
things. At coffee with a friend, I distractedly thought back
to a sugar jar that fascinated me as a child—a cut-glass bowl
divided in two parts, with a metal lid that never lay quite flat,
the light striking the glass and hovering oddly around it. I
liked to lift the lid and close it, lift it and close it; the act of
opening contained some piquant, totemic pleasure, and one

day the confluence of the thick, chewy glass and the radiant light invoked in me a baptismal shock: time was our master, and the world lay beyond our making. I kept opening and closing that bowl, until my mother, cooking dinner, snapped, *Enough with the sugar bowl.* Years later I saw these same bowls in Little Italy and wondered if my parents had palmed one from a restaurant back when they were first married—so poor, my father would laugh, that they used the Williamsburgh Savings Bank clock tower to tell the time. I found myself yearning for the sound of her voice: *Enough with the sugar bowl.*

This yearning is what I felt most strongly in the weeks after my mother died. I kept thinking of a night many years ago, when I took a late flight to Dublin, where I was going to live for six months. I was nineteen, and it would be the longest time I had ever been away from home; boarding the plane that hazy summer night, I was lit up with the prospect of making my way in a strange city, where no one knew me and I knew no one. At one a.m., I woke up disoriented in my seat. Out the window to my right flashed the aurora borealis. I had never seen anything so spectacular. The twisting lights in the sky evoked a spectral presence. I had a sudden, acute desire to turn around and go back—not just back to my parents in Brooklyn, but deep into my childhood, into my mother's arms holding me on those late nights when we would drive home from dinner at a neighbor's house in the country, and she would sing a lullaby and tell me to put my head on her warm shoulder, and I would sleep.

WE HAD no rules about what to do right after my mother died; in fact we were clueless—

"What do we do now?"

"Call the nurse."

"The nurse says to stay here."

—and so we sat with my mother's body, holding her hands. I kept touching the skin on her face, which was rubbery but still *hers*, feeling morbid as I did it, but feeling, too, that it was strange that I should think so. This was my mother. In the old days, didn't the bereaved wash the body as they said their goodbyes? I was ransacking the moment for understanding. Finally, when the funeral home workers came to take her body away, I went to my room and called some friends, saying, "My mother has died." I had the floating sensation that I was acting out a part in a movie, trying the words on.

Once my mother's body was gone, my father immediately moved the furniture back into place and wheeled the hospital bed onto the porch, where it assumed the bedraggled look of an outdated piece of machinery. He came back and sat down in his normal chair, and for a panicked moment I wondered if this was how he would treat my mother's memory. But his eyes were looking inside himself instead of out; he seemed shrunken in his chair.

"I want to cook Christmas dinner," he said.

What else was there to do? A few hours later Jim had

driven down from his parents' house to join us for dinner, and Liam's friend Emily had taken the train up from the city. I don't remember much about that dinner, except that we sat together, and there was carrot cake afterward, and it seemed odd to eat anything so sweet, and my father talked at one point about an enormous pig he and my mother had seen in Spain on their honeymoon, and I decided to fast for a day in recognition of this loss, which was so huge I needed to contain it somehow, to put barriers around its chaos. But the night slides away in my memory, like a balloon; there is no center to it. Do my brothers and my father remember those hours very differently? They must.

The next afternoon, my college friend Jodie came up; I was feverish. She took one look at me and brought me to the doctor. I hadn't slept a full night for a week or more, and I had a sinus infection. After she left, my high school boyfriend, M., came up with bagels and we went down to the basement rec room and watched TV for hours with my brothers. I was not sure if we were dead or alive. Would we, too, enter the world of the dead now? "Eating is a small, good thing at a time like this," says the baker to two newly bereaved parents in Raymond Carver's famous story. He feeds them rolls and dense, hearty bread and at last they talk; they cannot sleep, but the conversation and consumption bind them to this world.

My mother was cremated, and so we didn't have a proper funeral for her. At first my father didn't want to have any kind of funeral—just a memorial service, perhaps a month or two down the road.

"But she *died*," I said.

"I'm really exhausted, Meg," he said, looking drained. "I don't want to have to organize something and clean the house." I remonstrated with him and he said, "I'm *tired*," and went upstairs.

This resistance seemed bizarre to me. My mother had just died. And we weren't going to have a funeral for her because we were tired? I sat, unable to move, in the living room; though the furniture was back in place, the room seemed deflated and empty. A few minutes later my father came back downstairs.

"You're right," he said. "We should do this. It makes me anxious but I'll be OK."

I reminded him that we were the bereaved. We didn't have to provide the food. Someone would help us with it. And three days after my mother died, we gathered in our living room around pictures of her—I could barely look at the pictures of her as a young mother—and said our goodbyes. My father talked about how my mother, wanting to get out of the house a month or so before she died, had gone with him to return some books at the university library in New Haven; over lunch, afterward, she asked him, "Wouldn't it be nice if it could always be like this? If we weren't always worried about the things we had to get done?" My brothers and I, and her sisters and Isabel and Diana and even Diana's ten-year-old son all spoke briefly, too, and afterward, we all ate and drank and shared more stories of her life. My grandmother is normally a gregarious, optimistic person, but she didn't talk much. She looked very tired. Earlier, in the fall, my mother had said to me, "It's very hard for my mother to see me this sick. It'll be easier for her afterward." It didn't seem easier. Before my grandmother left, she pulled me aside in the foyer and said, "Just remember, your mother isn't with us anymore, but you kids carry her forward in this world. You all have her inside you."

The night blurred with exhaustion. I remember trying to eat the warm, cheesy pasta our friend Peter, a chef, had brought, and being unable to get the slippery pieces down my throat.

When I got back to Brooklyn, I didn't know what to do with myself. I couldn't focus on anything at first. Because of the holidays, most of my friends were away. I wasn't teaching that semester; I was still working on the Web magazine, which would launch in May, but I had a week's leave. The world seemed to push me away. I felt that I was pacing in the chilly dark outside a house with lit-up windows, wishing I could go inside. But I also felt that the people in those rooms were shutting out the news of a distant, important war, a war I had just returned from. Consumed by the question of what it means to be mortal, I looked around and thought, We are all going to die. When a friend talked about a minor problem at work, I wanted to shake her: You're healthy, your loved ones are healthy, this problem is small. I stared at the clock, willing the minutes to pass. I hated being alone. I hated time. One night I went out with M., my old boyfriend—we had been seeing each other, sort of; I had gravitated toward the solace of a shared past—and stayed out till six a.m., with no idea how late it was. I wanted the hours to rush past. I wanted to fast-forward a week, a month, a year to when I'd feel "better." Though I had been "prepared," I remained clueless about the rules of shelter and solace in this new world of exile. I said to myself at times that it was not worth continuing. Life ended in death, and usually in great suffering. Why wait around? My mother was gone; my husband and I had divorced; the man I'd been dating was no longer part of my life; and even M. seemed skittish and odd. There was at least one night when I lay in bed eyeing the bottle of sleeping pills. I opened it and spilled them all over the bedside table, where they shone like moons of another galaxy. I wanted someone to save me—I desperately wanted someone to save me with an all-consuming love, as in a movie.

What was most difficult was that I myself didn't know what to expect. How long would I feel like this? Would this yearning ever pass? And—did I want it to?

THOUGH I WAS EXHAUSTED, I had a hard time sleeping. The nights were long and hallucinatory; death seemed present in the room with me, an enemy to have it out with then and there. After several fruitless, insomniac nights, I gave up trying to sleep. Instead, I read, turning to books to understand what was happening to me.

I had been sent healing workbooks and Buddhist texts about how to die. I had been sent *On Grief and Grieving* and *On Death and Dying* and the Bible and memoirs about deaths of parents. I read nearly all of them; I was hungry for death scenes. C. S. Lewis's *A Grief Observed*, his slim account of the months after his wife's death from cancer, was the most evocative. Grief is paradoxical: you know you must let go, and yet letting go cannot happen all at once. The literature of mourning enacts that dilemma; its solace lies in the ritual of remembering the dead and then saying, *There is no solace,* and also, *This has been going on a long time.*

But the book I was most preoccupied with those first nights was *Hamlet.* I returned over and over to key speeches as if they were prayers or clues. I'd always thought of Hamlet's melancholy as existential. His sense that the world "is out of joint" came across as vague and philosophical, the dilemma of a depressive young man who can't stop chewing at big metaphysical questions. But now it seemed to me that Hamlet was moody and irascible in no small part because he is grieving: his father has just died. He is radically dislocated, stumbling through the days while the rest of the world acts as if nothing important has changed.

For the trouble is not just that Hamlet is sad; it is that everyone around him is unnerved by his grief. When Hamlet comes onstage, his uncle greets him with the worst question you can ask a grieving person: "How is it that the clouds still hang on you?" Hamlet's mother, Gertrude, tries to get him to see that his loss is "common." No wonder Hamlet is angry and cagey; he is told that how he feels is "unmanly" and unseemly. This was a predicament familiar to me. No one was telling me that my sadness was unseemly, but I felt, all the time, that to descend to the deepest fathom of it was somehow taboo. (As my dad said, "You have this choice when you go out and people ask how you're doing. You can tell the truth, which you know will make them really uncomfortable, or seem inappropriate. Or you can lie. But then you're lying.") I was struck, too, by how much of *Hamlet* is about the precise kind of slippage the mourner experiences: the difference between being and seeming, the uncertainty about how the inner translates into the outer, the sense that one is expected to *perform* grief palatably. (If you don't seem sad, people worry; but if you are grief-stricken, people flinch away from your pain.)

Hamlet also captures an aspect of loss I found difficult to speak about—the profound ennui, the moments of angrily feeling it is not worth continuing to live. In *A Grief Observed*, Lewis captures the laziness of grief, how it made him not want to shave or answer letters. Hamlet's famous soliloquy invokes that numb exhaustion:

> O that this too too sullied flesh would melt,
> Thaw, and resolve itself into a dew,
> Or that the Everlasting had not fix'd

127

> His canon 'gainst self-slaughter. O God! God!
> How weary, stale, flat, and unprofitable
> Seem to me all the uses of this world!

"Weary, stale, flat, and unprofitable": yes. I shared with Hamlet the pained wish that I might melt away.

Researchers have found that the bereaved are at a higher risk for suicidal thinking than the depressed. But Hamlet, I thought, is less searching actively for death than wishing futilely for the world to make sense again. And this, too, was how I felt.

I took a trip to California, to visit my friend Dana and go to the Mojave Desert for a few days. I needed a break, a different landscape; the holidays had hardly been a "vacation."

On my way to Joshua Tree National Park, a vast wind farm loomed on the left. The turning windmills were eerie, like machines from another world, and their strangeness made my stomach hurt with something like homesickness. The desert was dry and majestic and it calmed me; I was empty and it was, too. The open sky over the land, the juxtaposition of the minute and the majestic—it all expressed the dissonance I felt, and having my sense of smallness reflected back at me put me strangely at ease. How could my loss matter in the midst of all this? Yet it did matter to me, and in this setting that felt *natural*, the way the needle on the cactus in the huge desert is natural.

Hiking alone under the warm blue sky I had a sense that my mother was nearby—a vivid sensation I had had on several occasions since she died. I imagined I could detect her in the haze at the horizons, and so, for the first time since Christmas, I talked to her. I was walking along past the cacti, when I looked out into the rocky distance. "Hello, Mother," I whispered. "I miss you so much." Then I started crying. Ridiculously, I apologized. "I'm sorry. I don't want you to feel bad. I know you had to leave." I didn't want her to feel guilty that she couldn't be here with us.

A part of me knew this concern was foolish.

But it was intrinsic to the ritual, to the lingering belief that she was there, listening. I was powerless over it.

The solitude quickly turned painful. In a café, I ordered a coffee just so I didn't have to go back to my hotel room. In Brooklyn it had been hard to be around people, especially when they seemed uncomfortable talking about my mother, who was all I thought about. But it was also hard to be alone; one night, I spent hours writing to near strangers on Facebook, as if that would create the connection I was searching for.

I drove back to L.A. to see Dana. That night, we stayed up late, talking about the difficulty of grieving, its odd jags of ecstasy and pain. Dana's father had died several years earlier, and it was easy to speak with her: she belonged to what more than one acquaintance who's lost a parent has now referred to as "the club." It's not a club any of us wished to join, but it makes mourning less lonely. I told Dana that I felt my mother's loss was curiously unrecognized; I envied my

Jewish friends the ritual of saying Kaddish. She talked about the hodgepodge of traditions she had embraced in the midst of her grief. And then she asked me, "Have you found a metaphor?"

"A metaphor?"

"Have you found your metaphor for where your mother is?"

As she said it, I realized I had. It was the sky—the wind. The cynic in me cringed, but it was true.

I am the indoctrinated child of two lapsed Irish Catholics, which is to say, I am not religious. I was bothered when people offered up the—to me—empty consolation that whatever happened, my mother "will always be there with you." But when my mother died, I did not believe that she was gone. As she exhaled a last time, her face settled into repose. Her body grew still, but I felt she had simply been transferred into another substance; what substance, and where it might be located, I wasn't sure. I went onto my parents' porch without putting my coat on. The limp winter sun sparkled off the frozen snow on the lawn, and I asked the air to take good care of my mother. I addressed the fir tree she liked and the wind moving in it. "Please keep her safe for me."

Later, after talking to Dana, I asked Isabel whether she had a metaphor for where my mother was. She unhesitatingly answered: "The water. The ocean."

The idea that my mother might be *somewhere* rather than nowhere is hard for the skeptical empiricist in me to swallow. But there it is. At times I simply felt she was just on a long trip. I was reminded of an untitled poem by Franz Wright, which reads in full:

I basked in you;
I loved you, helplessly, with a boundless tongue-tied love.
And death doesn't prevent me from loving you.
Besides,
in my opinion you aren't dead.
(I know dead people, and you are not dead.)

At lunch one day, after flying home, as velvety snow coated the narrow Brooklyn streets, I tried to talk about this haunted feeling with a friend whose son died a few years ago. She told me that she, too, felt that her son was with her, and she frequently talked to him. She is an intellectually exacting person, and she said that she had sometimes wondered about how to conceptualize her persistent intuition. A psychiatrist reframed it for her: he said the people we most love do become a physical part of us, ingrained in our synapses, in the pathways where memories are created.

That was a kind of comfort. But I resisted the therapist's view. I needed to experience my mother's presence in the world *around* me and not just in my head. Every now and then, I saw a tree shift in the wind and its bend had, to my eye, a distinctly maternal cast. For me, my metaphor was—as all good metaphors ought to be—a persuasive transformation. In these moments, I did not say to myself that my mother was *like* the wind; I thought she *was* the wind. I felt her: there, and there.

One book about grief that I found convincing—and strangely consoling—was by Colin Murray Parkes, a British psychiatrist and a pioneer in bereavement research. Drawing on work by another researcher, John Bowlby, he argued that the dominant element of grief was a restless "searching." The heightened physical arousal, anger, and sadness of grief resemble the anxiety that children suffer when they're separated from their mothers. Parkes speculated that we likewise continue to "search" illogically (and in distress) for a loved one after a death. He states the mourner's predicament clinically and as clearly as anyone:

> In his heart of hearts he often believes that the dead do not return yet he is committed to the task of recovering one who is dead. It is no wonder that he feels that the world has lost its purpose, and no longer makes sense.

As we fail over and over to find the lost person, Parkes suggests, we slowly create a new world, the old one having been invalidated by death. It occurred to me that my metaphor finding was precisely this, a secular mind searching for its lost love.

One day, I sat up in shock when I felt my mother shake me out of a pervasive fearfulness that was making it hard for me to get on the subway. Whether it was the ghostly flicker of my synapses or an actual ghostly flicker of her spirit, I don't know. I would be lying if I said I wasn't hoping it was the latter.

IN THE FIRST WEEKS after my mother's death, I became intensely obsessed with M., my high school boyfriend. Partly it was that I craved the connection of sex; he had come to Connecticut after my mother's death and stayed the night, and the whole time I felt a weird nerviness around him. While we watched TV, I was formal and polite with him at first; I kept making sure there was some distance between us on the couch. I felt I could pull him into me, like a black hole, in my exhausted derangement, and this seemed unfair, inappropriate, indecorous. When I touched him then pulled away, he said, in a low voice, "That's right. God forbid you touch me."

The funeral was the next day. The prospect of it hung heavily at the edge of my mind.

"Do you want to stay in my room?" I asked.

"Whatever you want," he said.

What I wanted was to be demolished. I pulled him onto the bed, with the sensation of diving into deep black water. In the morning I was dressing for the funeral and he looked up from the bed, eyes still clouded with sleep, and said, "You look lovely," and for a moment it seemed the years had reeled back, and I was in high school.

M. and I had gone out my senior year. I met him when I was around the age at which my mother had met my father, and in the most infatuated, idyllic moments of our relationship, I fantasized that we, too, would run off and get married. At the end of my freshman year of college, though, I broke up with M.; I loved him, but I thought I was doing the wrong thing by keeping myself tied to someone far away. I had absorbed the idea that I was supposed to be independent, that I was supposed to explore, that I was growing up in an age of freedom for women. For years I thought of our relationship nostalgically, because in it I had known a kind of youthful joy and optimism that I never experienced as vibrantly again.

His reentrance into my life had intersected eerily with my mother's illness. We'd run into each other in a coffee shop the day I found out my mother's cancer had returned, and made plans to see each other. When we did, we talked nostalgically about our relationship and the curious vividness it had for both of us all these years later. There was still something between us, but everything was kept at bay for some time, until one fall night, not long before my mother died, he kissed me. He smelled the same, and I had the sensation of dropping into a vortex; the past was present.

Since then, there had been something ghostly about our encounters. In the time before her death he floated into my life, then disappeared, then came back again, and I did the same. But after the death, I suddenly wanted to clutch him close. After my mother's funeral, we had dinner a few times, and one night he came over when I called him in tears, and soothed me. But he always seemed to be holding back—why, I did not know. I fretted about this evasiveness, wishing that he would plunge into my grief with me, even though I knew that was unrealistic, unwise. When I talked to friends in those first weeks, I often talked about him, not my mother. By some strange internal math, he had become part of her disappearance: if I could hold on to, reconnect, with him, *she* might return. We could travel backward through time, and I could choose not to leave him, and my mother would still be alive. It was like an algebraic equation whose variables I couldn't keep straight. Even if I couldn't reclaim her, if I ended up with him, I might somehow *become* her—I could have a version of her life, her newly valuable, lost life.

One night, we went out to celebrate my birthday; unable to bear the odd intensity of my feelings, I said to him, after we'd gone to my apartment, that perhaps this was not the time to be seeing each other. I was in a strange place; I didn't want him to pity me or to be afraid to call things off if he wasn't interested. Inwardly I was hoping that he would assure me he wanted to be with me. And he did. Then he lifted me in the air and hugged me, and gave me a birthday present.

After this, he pretty much vanished. When I called, he didn't call back. Weeks passed. A few weeks later, he phoned to say he would be coming to the memorial service we were holding for my mother. At the service itself, he acted odd, avoiding me at the reception. Leaving early, he said, "We should talk." I raised an eyebrow, and he said, "I didn't mean it like that, I just meant I had to apologize for not calling sooner." But he never called.

You motherfucker, I thought. My mother died. Now

you're going to make it feel like you died, too—like every-thing I touch will disappear.

This second vanishing of someone I loved haunted me; it seemed so strangely *symbolic*.

I began to wonder if I had invented it. I began, too, to have dreams that he called to explain what had happened, why he had disappeared; in them, I experienced a curiously intense sense of relief.

It didn't occur to me at the time that these dreams were really about my mother, concocted, in the strange logic of the dreaming brain, to continue to make me think some reunion *was* possible. Later I read that the bereaved often focus on the first loss they ever endured rather than the loss they'd just suffered. I found that to be true. *M., M.,* I would pine, lying in bed at night, or taking a bath.

In February, there was a two-day snowstorm in New York. For hours I lay on my couch, reading, watching the snow drift down through the large elm outside, wondering what had happened to M., the sky going gray, then eerie violet, the night breaking around us, snow like flakes of ash. A white mantle covered trees, cars, lintels, and windows. It was like one of grief's moods: melancholic; estranged from the normal; in touch with the longing that reminds us that we are being-toward-death, as Heidegger puts it. Loss is our atmosphere; we, like the snow, are always falling toward the ground, and most of the time we forget it.

But grief left me perhaps too aware of the transience of everything. In its heightened moments I revered the world—light gracing the corner of a building, the wind on the beach. At other times, the awareness that everything disappears was nightmarish. On the second night of the blizzard, I slept restlessly, waking at three a.m. in a cold sweat, my heart racing. I had dreamed that I was walking up and down a dirt road overhung by ancient elms, dashing from the grasp of wraiths that were pursuing me, trying to make me one of them. The wraiths were evil, and it was my job to walk up and down the road and their job to envelop me. I couldn't sleep afterward; sometimes you can't make it better even with the lights on. It was hard in these moments to wake up utterly alone, to realize that both my marriage and my mother were truly gone.

ONE NIGHT, I was talking to my father on the phone when he mentioned a "loss of confidence" that we had all experienced. I asked him what he meant. I'd felt strangely off-balance and insecure since my mother died, but I'd always been nervous, especially compared with my brothers, and I was in the midst of reconstituting my life as a single person whose friends were mostly married and having babies. "Your mother is not there," he explained. "And we are dealing with her absence. It makes us feel, I think, a loss of confidence—a general loss, an uncertainty about what we can rely on."

I counted it as lucky that I did not have to work full-time in the first months after my mother's death. But helping launch the new Web magazine was intense work and demanded a level of focus that was beyond me. In the past, I had been good at keeping track of details, but now I couldn't. Often it took all my energy simply to get to the office, and at meetings I found it hard to concentrate. Instead, my brain ran through my mother's last days over and over. I intensely wanted to write down the story of her death or tell it, over and over, to friends; I read and reread the journal I'd kept during her illness.

I wasn't sure why, except that the habit of writing things down to understand them had been planted in me by her. When I was five, she gave me a red corduroy–covered notebook for Christmas. I sat in my floral nightgown turning the blank pages, wondering what on earth I was supposed to do with it.

What do I do with it?

You write down things that happened to you that day.

Why would I want to do that?

Because maybe they're interesting and you want to remember them.

What would I write?

Well, you'd write something like "Today I saw a woman with purple hair crossing Montague Street."

I still remember the way she said that sentence: *Today I saw a woman with purple hair crossing Montague Street.* It was one of those memories my mother gave me that I carried around, and always would, like the shard of a shell that falls out of a bag you took to the beach that long happy summer.

I hadn't seen a woman with purple hair crossing Montague Street, of course. But in that sentence was my mother's sense that one might want to capture the extraordinary, her intuitive grasp for children's love of the absurd, her striking physical *presence* (she was leaning toward me, backlit, her long hair falling toward and over me), her knowledge that my seriousness, already, needed to be leavened with playfulness.

I also felt that if I told the story of her death, I could understand it better, make sense of it—perhaps even change it. What had actually happened still seemed implausible: A person was present your entire life, and then one day she disappeared and never came back. It resisted belief. Even when a death is foreseen, I was surprised to find, it still feels sudden—an instant that could have gone differently.

If I could find a flaw in the story, I thought, if I could find the right turning point, then perhaps—like Orpheus—I could bring the one I sought back from the dead. *Aha: Here she is, walking behind me.* But some part of me understood I could not bring her back. The story of Orpheus, it now occurs to me, is not just about the living's desire to resuscitate the dead, but about the ways the dead drag us along into their shadowy realm because we cannot let them go. So we follow them into the Underworld, descending, until one day we turn, and return.

I saw my therapist twice a week for a while, though I had no money; she gave me a break. I looked forward to our sessions greedily. I was hungry for her time; I thought perhaps she could save me; I couldn't wait to get to her office because there, at least, I didn't have to feel self-conscious about my sorrow, my desire to talk about my mother, my need to tell the story of her death over. This was the gift of those sessions. Still, I nearly always left crestfallen. It wasn't my therapist's fault: there was no way for her to do what I wanted her to do, which was to bring my mother back. In some sense, I was looking for a medium, not a shrink.

Medication might have helped, of course, and there were times when I thought, *Just give me something to take the pain away.* I had many of the typical signs of depression. But my pain and sleeplessness, my lack of appetite one day, my overabundance of it the next—these were not the result of an aimless melancholy. They were because my mother was dead. And there was one key difference between my grief and depressions I'd suffered in the past: the world appeared to me in heightened, shimmering outlines, like a mirage. At times it seemed excruciatingly beautiful, a place I never wanted to leave. I hated that my mother couldn't see the snow or the sky anymore. And in the end, I kept coming back to a simple fact: My pain was caused by the absence of my mother. Did I want to deny this? Did I want to medicate it away? I did not.

I HAD DINNER with Liam in Brooklyn one night, and he told me he had been dreaming about our mother. He was comforted by this. I was envious. I was not dreaming about her, and my main fear, in those first days, was that I would forget what her face looked like. I had told M. this fear. He looked at me and said, "That's not going to happen." I didn't know how he could know, but I was comforted by his certainty.

A month later, the dreams started. They were not frequent, but they were powerful. Unlike dreams I'd had about my mother when she was alive, these seemed to capture her as she truly was, as if, in the nether realm of sleep, we actually were visiting each other. These visits were always full of boundaries: I was never fully able to grasp her.

In the first dream it was summertime, and my mother and I were standing outside a house like one we used to go to on Cape Cod. There was a sandy driveway and a long dirt road. We were going to get ice cream, and we were saying goodbye to Eamon, who was just a little boy. When I looked at him, an oceanic sadness filled me, but I didn't know why. He smiled and waved from the porch as we left; I was driving, which struck me as odd. I kept trying to turn to see my mother, but I had to keep my eyes on the road, so I couldn't see her clearly. It became evident she was going away, though I couldn't figure out where.

As we headed down the road, my mother talked about Eamon, telling me I didn't need to be anxious about him. The conversation replicated one we'd had while she was in the hospital, when she'd worried about dying when Eamon was still in college, and I had reassured her he would be OK; here, it was as if she were playing my role and I was playing hers. Every time I looked at her, a sadness filled me, one so cold and deep that even months later, when I thought of it, my heart sped up. It was like ice being poured down my windpipe.

The second dream had an even stronger quality of visitation. I was at my parents' house, feeling anxious about work. In the den, my father was watching football, and I told him I needed to go back to New York. As he got up to get the train schedule, I became aware in my peripheral vision that there were holiday ornaments on the kitchen table and that someone was sitting there. "Stay another night," I heard my mother's voice say, and I looked up to see that *she* was the person at the table. Her hands were busy—either knitting or rolling dough for apple pie. "Stay the night," she said again, with longing in her voice. "Of course," I said.

My father and Liam told me about their dreams, and the continuities among them startled me. Our dreams followed certain rules or patterns. In all, we knew either that my mother was gone or that something was wrong. In all, too, she was hard to reach, but we were given a moment to share a look with her. I still have these dreams, and every time I wake from them, I am reminded of those passages from epics in which the hero goes to the Underworld and sees his father but cannot embrace him. Or of the sonnet by Milton about his wife, who died in childbirth. Recounting a dream about her, he wrote, "Methought I saw my late espoused saint," and then described her disappearance at precisely the moment they tried to touch: "But oh! As to embrace me she inclin'd, / I wak'd, she fled, and day brought back my night."

What surprised me was how comforted I felt when I woke from the first dream. I was sad that it had ended, but it was not the depleted sadness I had often experienced when waking up from a wishful dream. It seemed my mother had been saying something important to me: I was still her daughter. I woke reassured, like a child who has kicked the covers off her in her sleep on a chilly night and dimly senses her mother steal into the dark room, pull them up over her, and stroke her hair before leaving.

Other nights, there were bad dreams, and I woke shaking.

Reading a library book one day, I found my eyes kept circling back up to a word someone had penciled in along the margin: *Gravestones. Gravestones.* There was nothing special about the word; the passage was about burial practices becoming more elaborate. Then I thought with queer excitement: My mother wrote that word! It was her handwriting! My brain backtracked: She had studied for a master's at NYU. I might have a book she read. And I started frantically flipping through the book, searching for more penciled words in her hand—as if they were messages left behind.

The idea that the dead might not be utterly gone has an irresistible magnetism. I'd read something that described what I had been experiencing. Many people go through what psychologists call a period of "animism," in which you see the dead person in objects and animals around you, and you construct your false reality, the reality where she is just hiding, or absent. This was the mourner's secret position, it seemed to me: *I have to say this person is dead, but I don't have to believe it.*

One psychologist whose work I consulted had written, "Bereaved people, driven by the pain and yearning of grief, imagine signs of communication." His cut-and-dried language did not convey how powerful that imagining could be. What words could I use to convey how much I wanted her back?

The night is very long and my mother is lost in it. I can see the world below the plane, the aurora borealis shifting to my right, just outside my field of vision, just beneath the surface of my consciousness, a cold sea, a bright star.

CHAPTER EIGHT

observing grief

One of the things I did after my mother died was talk to people who might help me make sense of my grief. Among them was a woman named Holly Prigerson, a clinical researcher on grief at the Dana-Farber Cancer Institute at Harvard, who told me something that has stayed with me: When a terminally ill patient "accepts" her death, the bereaved typically find their grief more manageable than when a terminally ill patient is in "despair" about her death. It is, of course, difficult to study "grief" because a salient feature of grief is that it's not monolithic or singular; it's personal and variable. That said, there seem to be certain universal aspects. And one is this ameliorating influence of watching your loved one accept his or her death. (Another is that the dominant feeling after a loss isn't anger or denial but yearning, exactly the feeling I'd had.)

Needless to say, witnessing the acceptance is painful in its own right. I thought about all the Buddhist books that had been recommended to me after my mother's death, among them Gehlek Rimpoche's *Good Life, Good Death* and Sogyal Rinpoche's *The Tibetan Book of Living and Dying*. These books stress the importance of accepting the impermanence of life. At times, this notion (as filtered through Western self-help) strikes me as cruelly sanctimonious—you routinely encounter the story of the angry cancer-riddled woman who consults a monk, learns to accept her death and attend to her spiritual needs, and, voilà!, is healed. But I take to heart what a book like *Good Life, Good Death* has to say about what acceptance and a "good death" might be, even if its ideas are not novel: Gehlek Rimpoche counsels mainly acknowledgment of what is taking place and a letting go on the part of both the ill and the soon-to-be-bereaved.

This is good advice, but not every temperament is able to heed it. Acceptance isn't necessarily something you can choose off a menu, like eggs instead of French toast. Instead, researchers now think that some people are inherently primed to accept their own death with "integrity" (their word, not mine), while others are primed for "despair." Most of us, though, are somewhere in the middle, and one question researchers are now focusing on is: How might more of those in the middle learn to accept their deaths? The answer has real consequences for both the dying and the bereaved. For one thing, the terminally ill make clearer decisions about their end-of-life medical care when they have acknowledged their impending death; for another, watching them acknowledge their death helps us, in turn, accept it, too. Cancer is not a gentle disease, and my family and I witnessed my mother in traumatic, painful moments we might all rather forget. But in this one regard, at least, my mother had what Buddhists and psychologists would call a good death. Which is to say: She accepted it that day in the hospital when the doctor told her she was going to die.

Later that day, her four sisters and her mother came to say goodbye. My mother sat in the living room of her hospital suite, with her legs poking out from her hospital pants. She and her sisters sat and joked and reminisced. My mother had been nervous about the visit beforehand, but now she relaxed. One sister asked my mother what her favorite color was. (Blue.) My grandmother was quiet. At one point, she gave my mother a garden angel and a piece of paper. "I couldn't sleep last night," she said. "And in the middle of the night I remembered this prayer I had taped above your bed when you were a little girl, and I wrote it down for you." My mother often bridled at religious gestures but now she didn't. She read the prayer and said, "I remember this. I'll put it by my bed."

Overwhelmed, I went back to the house to take a run and to let them be together. When I returned, my mother was alone, sitting in bed, looking contemplative.

"Hi, Mom," I said. (How many more times will I say that, I wondered.)

"Wasn't that nice?" she said.

I sat at the end of the bed and gave her a foot massage, which I did a lot in those last three weeks—it helped take her mind off her pain, which increased every day, and gave me something to do. "I thought so," I said. "That's why I left for a while."

"It *was* nice," she said. "We laughed a lot. I want them to remember me with a sense of humor." She grew quiet. "It was hard to say goodbye to them." She paused and stared at her hands. She had begun to have a pronounced inward quality, a withdrawn beauty, as if she were already on her way to another world. "But not the way you'd think." Then she looked at me and said, "It's good to have time to contemplate the end of your life. I mean, when else do you do it? When do you really think about death?"

"It *is* good?" I asked, as I rubbed lotion into her cracked soles.

"It's not what I would have thought," she said. "I'm not afraid. I feel I will still be here." Then she began to talk about what she wanted in her last days. She wanted her hospital bed to be in the living room, so she could look out the picture window at things that "would last a long time." She wanted to look at the fir tree on the lawn. And the pond. Just that year, a great blue heron had made a habit of stopping in the pond to fish. We would see him rise up out of the water, his wingspan at once awkward and magnificent. It was nearly Christmas, and she wanted us to buy a tree to be in the room with her bed. She talked about my brothers, and my dad, and said again that she wasn't afraid, though she was sad about "sappy" things.

"Like what?"

"Like Christmas. And my birthday." I took some lavender oil and put it behind her ears. She tilted her chin up so I could sweep her hair back. She loved lavender, and it was supposed to be calming. "I'm sad about the things I have a lot of memories of, of the days when the whole family was together," she continued. "That's why I'm sad about Christmas and my birthday."

I began to cry. Through tears, I said, "I'm going to miss you so much." I expected that she would get tears in her eyes or melt in that special way that mothers melt—or, at least, that *she* usually melted when she saw one of us kids in pain. Instead, she looked at me and said, "I know," with a quiet calm. She had a funny look on her face, a look I had never quite seen directed at me, of appraisal and remove. In that moment, I had the sense that she was letting me know something, that she thought I would be OK. Even if we both felt the moment had come too soon, this was what happened: Parents died, while children lived, and in some sense it was meant to be. It was not the response I wanted, but the authority of her look stilled me. I wiped away my tears. "I know," she said again.

Now, in the worst moments, my mind often goes back to that night in the hospital. I think of when she said, "I know," and it calms me. Her voice had the strange motherly knowledge that nothing approximates.

"I don't want anyone to be afraid to ask me questions," she told me. We had no idea that three days later she would lapse back into a coma-like state and never speak again. How could we? Even in the midst of acceptance, we were always bargaining for more time. We still lived inside Zeno's paradox—the idea that if you go halfway toward something over and over, you never actually arrive.

A death from a long illness is different from a sudden death. It gives you time to say goodbye and time to adjust to the idea that the beloved will not be with you anymore. Some researchers have found it is "easier" to experience a death if you know for at least six months that your loved one is terminally ill. But this fact is like orders of infinity: there in theory, hard to detect in practice. On my birthday, a friend mused out loud that my mom's death had surely been easier to bear because I had known it was coming. I almost bit her head off: *Easier to bear compared to what—the time she died of a heart attack?* Instead, I bit my tongue.

What studies actually said was that I would begin to "accept" my mother's death more quickly than I would have in the case of a sudden loss—possibly because I experienced "anticipatory grief" while she was still alive. But until that acceptance arrived, it was as hard to bear as any other major loss.

And that was why one afternoon, about three weeks after my mother died, unable to get far from bed, I googled "grief." I was having a bad day. It was two p.m., and I was on the bed wondering: Was it normal to believe surviving was pointless? Was I losing my mind? I wanted a picture of this experience from the outside: a clinical picture. So I began to read, thinking that information might stop me from feeling that I was floating away.

Not surprisingly, perhaps, the clinical literature on grief is extensive. Much of it reinforces what I had already begun to realize. Grief isn't rational; it isn't linear; it is experienced in waves. "No one ever told me that grief felt so like fear," C. S. Lewis had written at the beginning of *A Grief Observed*, and scientists have in fact found that grief, like fear, is a stress reaction, attended by deep physiological changes. Levels of stress hormones like cortisol increase. Sleep patterns are disrupted. The immune system is weakened. Mourners may experience loss of appetite, palpitations, even hallucinations. Just as I had, they sometimes imagine that the deceased has appeared to them, in the form of a bird, say, or a cat. Addressing my mother in the sky was not as bizarre as I'd thought; mourners often talk out loud—or cry out—to a lost one, I found. Freud theorized that the reason for all this distress has to do with energy. In his essay "Mourning and Melancholia," he suggests that mourners have to reclaim the energy they have invested in the deceased loved one. Grieving is that process of reclamation. When you lose someone you were close to, you have to reassess your picture of the world and your place in it. The more your identity is wrapped up with the deceased, the more difficult the mental work.

The first systematic survey of grief, I read, was conducted by Erich Lindemann. Having studied 101 people, many of them related to the victims of the Cocoanut Grove fire of 1942, he defined grief as "sensations of somatic distress occurring in waves lasting from twenty minutes to an hour at a time, a feeling of tightness in the throat, choking with shortness of breath, need for sighing, and an empty feeling in the abdomen, lack of muscular power, and an intensive subjective distress described as tension or mental pain." Intensive subjective distress. Yes, exactly: that was the objective description I was looking for. The experience is, as Lindemann notes, brutally physiological. It literally takes your breath away. Its physicality is also what makes grief so hard to communicate to anyone who hasn't experienced it.

One of the questions I had was whether there was any empirical evidence supporting the famous "five stages of grief." Mention that you had a death in the family to anyone, stranger or friend, and he is likely to say something about the five stages. According to "stage theory," an idea popularized by Elisabeth Kübler-Ross in her famous 1969 study *On Death and Dying*, grieving typically takes the form of five emotional stages, in sequence: denial, anger, bargaining, depression, and acceptance. This idea took hold in American culture almost as soon as Kübler-Ross articulated it (even though originally she used it to describe the grief the *dying* feel), perhaps because it makes loss sound controllable—and because the idea of acceptance appeals to our national character. In the months after my mother died, I saw stage theory invoked repeatedly, especially on TV medical shows. But my experience seemed to bear little resemblance to the "stages," and as it turns out, stage theory isn't a very accurate description of what it's like to grieve. There is little evidence suggesting that most people experience capital-letter Denial, Anger, Bargaining, Depression, and Acceptance in simple sequence. Instead, according to a study that Prigerson, the Dana-Farber researcher, worked on, Kübler-Ross's stages seem to be more like states. Though Kübler-Ross captured the range of emotions that the dying and their families experience, grief doesn't generally follow a checklist. It's less like an orderly progression of stages and more like an ongoing, messy process—sometimes one that never fully ends.

One of the things Prigerson told me when I talked to her on the phone was that researchers now believe there are two kinds of grief: "normal grief" and "complicated grief" (also called "prolonged grief"). "Normal grief" is a term for what most bereaved people experience. It peaks within the first six months and then begins to dissipate. "Complicated grief" does not, and often requires medication or therapy. But even "normal grief," Prigerson said, is hardly gentle. Its symptoms include insomnia or other sleep disorders, difficulty breathing, auditory or visual hallucinations, appetite problems, and dryness of mouth. I had had all of these symptoms, including one banal hallucination at dinner with a friend, when I imagined I saw a waitress bring him ice cream. In addition to the symptoms Prigerson named, I had one more: difficulty spelling. Like my mother, I had always been a good speller. Now I had to rely on the dictionary to ascertain whether *siege* is spelled *ie* or *ei*. My problem was not unusual; certain forms of grief can take a toll on your cognitive functions.

An enduring psychiatric idea about grief is that the

mourner needs to "let go" in order to "move on," and in the weeks after my mother died, people kept suggesting as much. But I didn't want to let go. And in fact studies have shown that some mourners hold on to a relationship with the deceased with no notable ill effects. In China, for instance, mourners regularly speak to dead ancestors, and one study demonstrated that the bereaved there "recovered more quickly from loss" than bereaved Americans do.

I wasn't living in China, though, and in those weeks after my mother's death, I felt that the world expected me to absorb the loss and move forward, like some kind of emotional warrior. One night I heard a character on *24*—the president of the United States—announce that grief was a "luxury" she couldn't "afford right now." This model represents an old American ethic of muscling through pain by throwing yourself into work; embedded in it is a desire to avoid looking at death. We've adopted a sort of "Ask, don't tell" policy. The question "How are you?" is an expression of concern, but as my dad had said, the mourner quickly figures out that it shouldn't always be taken for an actual inquiry. Around this time I read a book by a Johns Hopkins researcher in which she described an exchange, three months after her husband's death, with a colleague who asked her to peer-review an article. The researcher said, "My husband just died." To which her colleague responded, "It's been three months." A mourner's experience of time isn't like everyone else's. Grief that lasts longer than a few weeks may look like self-indulgence to those around you. But if you're in mourning, three months seems like nothing—going by Prigerson's research, three months might well find you approaching the height of sorrow.

My pervasive loneliness was a result, I believe, of what I now think of as the privatization of grief. For centuries, private grief and public mourning were allied in most cultures. In many places, it used to be that if your husband died the village came to your door, bearing fresh-baked rolls or soup. As Darian Leader, a British psychoanalyst, argues in *The New Black: Mourning, Melancholia, and Depression*, mourning—to truly be *mourning*—"requires other people." To lose someone was to be swept into a flurry of rituals. In many nations some kind of viewing followed the cleaning of the body—what was known as a wake in Ireland, an "encoffining" in China. Many cultures had—and some still have—special mourning clothes. In the Jewish shiva, a mourner sits on a low chair and is visited by friends and family. In *The Hour of Our Death*, a magisterial history of Western attitudes toward mortality, which Isabel had given me, Philippe Ariès notes that until the turn of the twentieth century, "the death of a man still solemnly altered the space and time of a social group that could be extended to include the entire community."

Why, I wondered, did I live in a world where there were so few rituals to guide me through this loss? The British anthropologist Geoffrey Gorer, the author of *Death, Grief, and Mourning*, argues that, at least in Britain, the First World War played a huge role in changing the way people mourned. Communities were so overwhelmed by the sheer number of dead that the practice of ritualized mourning for the individual eroded. Other changes were less obvious but no less important. More people, including women, began working outside the home; in the absence of caretakers, death increasingly took place in the quarantining swaddle of the hospital. The rise of psychoanalysis shifted attention from the communal to the individual experience. In 1917, only two years after Émile Durkheim wrote about mourning as an essential social process, Freud's "Mourning and Melancholia" defined it as something essentially private and individual, internalizing the work of mourning. Within a few generations, I read, the experience of grief had fundamentally changed. Death and mourning had been largely removed from the public realm. By the 1960s, Gorer could write that many people believed that "sensible, rational men and women can keep their mourning under complete control by strength of will and character, so that it need be given no public expression, and indulged, if at all, in private, as furtively as . . . masturbation." Today, our only public mourning takes the form of watching the funerals of celebrities and statesmen. It's common to mock such grief as false or voyeuristic ("crocodile tears," one commentator called mourners' distress at Princess Diana's funeral), and yet it serves an important social function. It's a more mediated version, Leader suggests, of a practice that goes all the way back to soldiers in *The Iliad* mourning with Achilles for the fallen Patroclus.

I found myself nodding in recognition at Gorer's conclusions. "If mourning is denied outlet, the result will be suffering," Gorer wrote. "At the moment our society is signally failing to give this support and assistance. . . . The cost of this failure in misery, loneliness, despair and maladaptive behavior is very high." Maybe it's not a coincidence that in Western countries with fewer mourning rituals, the bereaved report more physical ailments in the year following a death.

After my mother died, I kept thinking, "I just want somewhere to put my grief." I was imagining a vessel for it: a long, shallow wooden bowl, irregularly shaped. I had the sense that if I could chant, or rend my clothes, or tear my hair, I could, in effect, create that vessel in the world. Five days after my mother died a man elbowed me aside on the subway and I felt bruised and angry; if I had been wearing mourning clothes, I furiously thought, he would have taken greater care. I longed for rituals not only to indicate I was still in mourning but also to have a nonpsychological way of commemorating and expressing my loss. Without ritual, the only way to share a loss was to talk about it—foregrounding the particularities of my own emotions, my own bereavement. At times, though, this sharing felt invasive. I did not want to be pitied. In those moments, I wanted a way to show my grief rather than tell it.

One reason people over the ages have ritualized grief is to perform it and thereby descant it. For most of human history, as Robert Pogue Harrison shows in *The Dominion of the*

Dead, elaborate rituals surrounding death served both to express and limit its power over our minds. "By expressing grief in the various forms of celebration or cult of the dead," the Italian philosopher Benedetto Croce writes, "one overcomes heartbreak, rendering it objective." Ritual helps us let go of our identification with the dead. In this way, ritual can contain what Robert Pogue Harrison calls the "crisis" of grief, so that the mourner doesn't plunge into "sheer delirium." All this clarified to me what I had been craving: a *formalization* of grief, one that might externalize it.

For I had some understanding of delirium. At my nadir, on a wintry night after my mother died, I opened up the cut on my arm—the cut I'd given myself at Thanksgiving. My entire mind and body hurt. Watching TV and eating dinner, I'd started to weep violently, almost as if someone had knocked the wind out of me. With my nails pressing deeply into the skin, I scraped open my inner arm. The flesh turned pink. I took an ivory-handled dinner knife on the plate beside me and dragged it along the healing scar. Red drops of blood welled up. It's hard to describe this now, because putting it in words seems to sensationalize it, or to devalue it. I did not want to hurt myself, or to die. I just wanted to create some embodiment of the heartbreak eating me up. And, oddly enough, it was clarifying. As soon as I did it, I thought: I need to get away for a bit. I went back to the desert, near Marfa, Texas, and while there I bought a black-and-white friendship bracelet to signify my loss, and I wore it for three months, never taking it off.

. . .

The disappearance of mourning rituals affects everyone, not just the mourner. One of the reasons many people are unsure about how to act around a loss is that they lack rules or meaningful conventions, and they fear making a mistake. Rituals used to help the community by giving everyone a sense of what to do or say. Now, we're at sea. My friend D.'s best friend had recently lost her husband; D. was anxious to feel that there was something she could *do* to help that didn't seem to diminish or trivialize her friend's pain.

Even so, ritual mourning does not appeal to everyone, I know. A friend raised her eyebrows when I said how drawn I was to the idea of public mourning. "I just went to my uncle's funeral," she said, "and I was horrified by the way some of the women who knew him least were wailing the most. It was hypocritical. The whole funeral seemed stale and false." Perhaps. But, I said, those women were also mourning their own prior losses, and this is in part what such rituals are for. They aren't just about the individual; they are about the community.

I got my own taste of this at a memorial service we held for my mother at Saint Ann's at the end of February. The service was held at the church around the corner, where we used to have choral concerts, and where the school's graduation ceremonies were held; the last time I'd been there was for Eamon's graduation. It was a cold, clear day, and when we arrived the church was nearly full. My father, my brothers, and I spoke, along with Isabel and Diana and a few of my mother's close friends. I felt nervous about speaking, but also strangely subdued; I kept looking around, seeing people from my childhood—a woman who'd been the assistant teacher in one of my mother's early second-grade classes; students my mother had taught when I was in kindergarten. The charge of contact I felt at seeing old faces carried more weight than I'd expected. What I actually said about my mother barely captured anything about her, or our relationship, but the coming together of all these people gave me a sense of solace. Even seeing them cry opened up a knot in me: my mother's death meant something to them. Students from the school where my mother worked sobbed so loudly that later my friends told me they were taken aback. But I understood the sobbing. They were putting their grief *into* the service. A few months later I was talking to my friend Katie, whose father had died after a long illness, and she said that it had been comforting to see other people cry at her father's memorial service. "It sounds strange or awful to say," she told me, "but my brother and I would poke each other and say, 'See that person? See how sad he is?' It made us feel part of a community of mourners."

It is human to want our friends and family to recover from pain, to look for a silver lining—or so I reminded myself. But when people stop mentioning the dead person's name to you, the silence can seem worse than the pain of hearing those familiar, beloved syllables. Henry James, after the death of his sister, Alice, and his friend James Russell Lowell, wrote in his journal: "The waves sweep dreadfully over the dead—they drop out and their names are unuttered." I thought of the famous letter Abraham Lincoln had sent to the woman who lost all her sons in the Civil War; while he wanted to tell her what a gift her sons had given to the nation, he also wrote that he did not want to "beguile" her out of her grief. Likewise, I wanted my distress acknowledged, rather than beguiled away with promises that one day I'd "heal" or "move on."

The painful fact behind every ritual and psychological finding is that even a "good" death is rarely good for the survivors. The word *grief,* I read in my etymological dictionary, derives from an old French word meaning "to burden." For this reason, the matter-of-fact mordancy of Emily Dickinson, the supreme poet of grief, provided more balm to me than did the glad tidings of those who talked about how death can enrich us. In her poem "I Measure Every Grief I Meet," the speaker's curiosity about other people's grief ends up conveying how heavy her own is:

I wonder if It weighs like Mine—
Or has an Easier size.

I wonder if They bore it long—
Or did it just begin—

I could not tell the Date of Mine—
It feels so old a pain—

I wonder if it hurts to live—
And if They have to try—
And whether—could They choose between—
It would not be—to die—

CHAPTER NINE

spring

It was a cold spring. A bitter rain came down for days on end, as if the gods knew my sorrow. In literary criticism, the term for this association is "pathetic fallacy," coined by the art critic John Ruskin to describe the attribution of human emotions to nature and inanimate objects; the harsh, angry moors in *Wuthering Heights* mirror the characters' lives. At work on the website, I was often irritable, and I'd decided that after its launch I would take the summer off, then go back to teaching. I couldn't fall asleep until late in the night. When I did sleep, I had violent dreams about people I loved. I dreamed that a friend told me I was doing a bad job at work; furious, I tore out a clump of her long blond hair.

This friend had been nothing but kind to me after my mother's death.

In a different dream, I got angry at a friend who told me that I had forgotten to prepare a presentation for her class. *You have no idea what this is like,* I wept. *My mother died. My mother died.*

My *mother* died.

In the dreams, when I said this, I experienced the shock all over again: My mother had died. It was hard to take it *in*; she was the very being who once contained me. As Adrienne Rich wrote, a mother is "beyond the verbally transmitted lore of female survival—a knowledge that is subliminal, subversive, preverbal: the knowledge flowing between two alike bodies, one of which has spent nine months inside the other." When you separate a puppy from its mother temporarily, it goes into protest mode; when you separate it from its mother permanently, it goes into despair. We need love and security as children, or else we wither.

Another psychoanalyst, René Spitz, wrote about a mini-epidemic of orphans becoming sickly in the 1940s. It turned out that, caught up in the new mania for hygiene, orphanages were no longer handling or playing with babies; they merely fed them and kept them warm and clothed. Many of the babies grew sick and some died. All had become much more susceptible to the very infections the hygienic approach was supposed to protect them from. (An allegory for mourning: The more we hygienically avoid messy emotions, the more they infect us?) It was from this work that John Bowlby developed his concept of attachment theory—the idea that infants are born with "an instinctive behavioral bond with mothers. That bond produces distress when a mother is absent, as well as the drive for the two to seek each other out when the child is frightened or in pain." You find the same process in other young mammals, "who also cry and cling and seek out their mothers when danger looms."

"The thing is," Liam kept saying, "she's the one who made me better when I felt like this. And that only makes this worse."

Around Easter, I began to experience some respite from my sorrow. The daffodils were peeking up out of the seemingly still-frozen ground. The magnolias had come into bloom, their spoon-size petals opening wide. And I started feeling less beset. Not "recovered." But more even-keeled. In this, I conformed to the clinical norm: many mourners begin to feel less depressed around four months after the death. (A part of me was annoyed: I didn't want to conform to a chart.) The main difference was that I had more energy; still, when I was sad, the pangs were just as painful—perhaps more so, since it had been longer since I've seen my mother, and the reality of her death was beginning to intrude in new ways.

Some researchers say grief comes in waves, welling up and dominating one's emotional life, then subsiding, only to recur—an experience I recognized as my own. As George A. Bonanno, a clinical psychologist at Columbia University, has written, "When we look more closely at the emotional experiences of bereaved people over time, the level of fluctuation is nothing short of spectacular." This oscillation, he theorizes, offers relief from the stress grief creates. That made sense. I thought of one of the lines from Lewis's *A Grief Observed*: "Sorrow . . . turns out to be not a state but a process," he wrote. "It needs not a map but a history."

Easter itself was terrible. I spent the day being reminded of the ghosts of Easters past: the many times my mother would hide eggs and then forget where she had put that last one. A week later, moldy and soft, it would turn up in someone's shoe. (At the time, I couldn't understand how she could forget: those precious eggs!) I walked around my quiet neighborhood, pained by the sight of parents and their children sauntering about in lazy togetherness.

The truth was that even four months after my mother's death, I still privately believed she was coming back. Deep down, I felt that—like Dr. Manhattan in *Watchmen*—she would, through some effort of mind, reconstitute herself and appear to me, even as a ghostly form.

On one of those warm spring days that come and vanish, I went for a run in Prospect Park. I finished the loop after a long hill near the entrance. At the top of the rise, there is a stand of magnolias and a view of what's called the Long Meadow. Exhausted, I sat on the grass and granted myself ten minutes to put aside the to-do lists invading my head and think. (One downside of feeling better had been that it was easier to pretend I was OK. Then work I couldn't do would pile up.) I felt the sun on my face. The grass tickled my hands. An ant crossed my pinkie.

As I relaxed, I thought of first one memory of my mother in this park, then another, and then, like a BlackBerry that has tuned in to its signal after a long flight, I was flooded by a dozen distinct memories of being with my mother here. There was the August day in 1994 when she and I met Diana, and we sat in the grass; I read books for school as they talked about their summers. There were the many mornings my mother and I would go running together in the park before school. We listened to running tapes we made and traded; we talked. One morning she had told me that her younger sister—who had a new baby—had colon cancer. Running in the cool air, I imagined myself to be her friend as well as her daughter.

So I sat there, thinking of her and looking around. I had for a moment the distinct feeling that she had asked me to do this—that she had said, somehow: I can't look at it; will you look for me? And as I sat, a robin hopped toward me. Its red breast was shiny, and it had bright, bold eyes. And I thought: OK, so, resurrection; I don't know. But what in the world—in the universe—made this creature? Can evolution account for the mystery of life? As a theory, it doesn't go as far as I'd like toward explaining the world. I wanted the sky to open up and reveal universal secrets to me. My whole life, I had been taught to read and study, to seek understanding in knowledge of history, of cultures. And here I was, ready to learn! But: silence. A robin hopping closer. I watched it for some time, half wondering if in any way it could be my mother. What MADE you, robin? my mind practically shouted. Then the bird lost interest in me. I stood up. I brushed the dirt from my pants and jogged out of the park, thinking about that bird. How could I disregard the bubbly, foolish sense of beauty I felt looking at it? And: How could I reconcile that with the pain my mother endured before she died?

The poet Anne Carson wrote that after her mother died she suddenly felt that everything she read was in ~~strike-through font~~. I understand what she meant. I write and want to strikethrough. I smile and want to strikethrough. It is as if, for some time, the world exists mostly in strikethrough. Over time, the strikethrough gets lighter, and you can see the words underneath more clearly. But it's still ~~there~~.

It's easy, when you're grieving, to resent your suffering. My grief was not ennobling me. It made me at times vulnerable and self-absorbed, needy and standoffish, knotted up inside, even punitive. I wanted a way to understand it. But it was hard to know what that way was outside of the ethical framework of religion. In the fall before my mother died, I'd copied out a passage from an interview in *The Paris Review* with the novelist Marilynne Robinson that gave me some solace. The interviewer recalled Robinson's having once observed that Americans tend to avoid contemplating "larger issues." Here is what Robinson, who is a practicing Protestant, said in response:

> The ancients are right: the dear old human experience
> is a singular, difficult, shadowed, brilliant experience

that does not resolve into being comfortable in the world. The valley of the shadow is part of that, and you are depriving yourself if you do not experience what humankind has experienced, including doubt and sorrow. We experience pain and difficulty as failure instead of saying, I will pass through this, everyone I have ever admired has passed through this, music has come out of it, literature has come out of it. We should think of our humanity as a privilege.

I was trying to learn to do that, because the otherworldliness of loss was so intense that at times I had to believe it was a singular passage, a privilege of some kind, even if all it left me with was a clearer grasp of our human predicament. It was why I kept finding myself drawn to the remote desert: I wanted to be reminded of how the numinous impinges on ordinary life. It was a sensation one could experience even in New York, but the hubbub of commerce and honking cars made it hard to let it in.

Late on the long days of winter and early spring I would often call Jim, craving the company of someone who knew me well; we fell into a routine of occasionally watching a movie or eating dinner together, but he embodied a future that had been forever lost, painfully discarded, and, stricken, I sometimes turned distant and cold even when I most craved his kindness. I wondered if this was bad for both of us—"Do you think maybe you should take a break from talking?" a friend asked—but contemplating not talking to him was like contemplating not taking a medicine I depended on.

ONE OF THE FEW TIMES my mother had sounded happy in the last spring of her life, the spring of 2008, during her fifth month of a second round of chemo, was when she talked about the landscaping plans she and my father had for their new home. It was the second home they'd owned. The first was our apartment in Brooklyn, four flights up. At last she had the yard she had always wanted. And at lunch one day—after we had gone to see the doctor who passed crystals over her body—my mother told me about the landscaper's first visit. "We're going to have staggered trees lining the driveway, so it's not too fussy. And we're planting irises and foxgloves at the top, where the drive ends abruptly; it looks like a parking lot right now. And we looked at trees to plant beside the pond by the road. I really want two weeping cherries. They're like weeping willows, but they have light pink blossoms. They're beautiful. But they're way too much money. Ten thousand dollars each." She played with her chopsticks. "Anyway, it's too late in the season," she said. "Maybe next year."

A few weeks later, I drove her home from New York-Presbyterian after her chemo. I was late to pick her up because I had wanted to squeeze in a run beforehand. She had an appointment with the doctor after chemo. I played the odds, guessing that he wouldn't see her right away. But I lost the gamble and she had to wait for me for ten minutes, standing weakened outside the hospital, her overstuffed bag drooping from her shoulder. When I looked at her settling exhaustedly into the car, her face scaly and dry from Erbitux, one of her cancer drugs, I thought, "Well, I'll just figure out how to *buy* her the cherry tree." As if I had the money.

She slept most of the way, waking only as we neared the house. "Look," she suddenly said. "There's one." And there it was: a swooping blast of pink among the bracken.

Now, a year later, there was a weeping cherry practically in my own front yard. I'd moved to my apartment the previous fall, just as my mother entered her final decline. I hadn't realized that my street was lined with flowering trees: wisteria, dogwood, and the pink weeping cherry. I experienced a shock every time I saw its drifting pink tendrils. Sometimes I thought that its presence meant my mother was coming back. Why would it be here unless it was to announce the universe's mistake? *Here you go. She's a good woman. You can have her a bit longer.*

I visited my father's house in mid-April. It was only the fourth time I had been there.

My father's house resembled my parents' house: same number of rooms, same smells of garlic and ginger in the kitchen, same dogs wagging their tails. It was what *wasn't* there that made it different. An absence that becomes a presence, like the shadow cast by an oil lamp on a stormy night: her voice, calling out to me as she went to bed, walking past my room, sometimes knocking and tucking her head around the corner: *Good night, Meg.* Her bustling around the kitchen, her coughing, her shuffling slippers, the way she sat in the mornings, those last five months, in the living room, looking out the window at the pines. Her solitude within herself. These things were missing. I had memories of her, but I no longer had her secret sense of the world, the self that took notes and wrote them in scraps of small books. I found one after she died, complaining that at Christmas my father had given her books she wouldn't be very interested in.

Dad showed me around the garden. He was excited. "Come see," he said. "Last year, your mother and I planted these irises and foxgloves. The irises never bloomed and I thought, oh well, they didn't take. Look at them now. The foxgloves were all brown and shriveled. I was about to dig them up a few weeks ago, when I came out and I found that they had grown several inches. And were green!" He was happy, as if this meant that my mother might, too, go green in the earth, and somehow return. It hurt to see how happy he was, and to think of them together, privately planting these flowers; the thought of his pain was too difficult for me to bear.

That weekend, I found one of my scrawled notes from a doctor's appointment my mother and I went to together:

Alkaline. Mushrooms.

It meant she needed to eat more alkaline foods, to combat the cancer.

The psychologist and bereavement expert Therese Rando argues that mourning requires people to recollect and re-experience the deceased before relinquishing the old attachments. I knew that I was supposed to relinquish the old attachment, but I didn't want to yet. When I see the lilacs my mother loved, I thought, will that not return her to me?

My father, I could tell as he showed me the flowers, was wondering something similar.

Last week, a friend e-mailed me about the cherry blossom festival at the Brooklyn Botanic Garden, which my parents had taken us to every spring as kids, and I decided to go, because my mother couldn't. I went on an unseasonably warm day—freak weather that descended on the Northeast for a weekend, sending us from spring to summer overnight. Entering the gardens was like walking into an old dream. The space was familiar, but I couldn't attach a narrative to it. I followed the flow of people past the front lawn, noting the benches and trees dedicated in memory of someone. I'd never understood the point of such benches. Now I did. (One day in college, I was sitting on a bench in my dorm's courtyard, when an old man approached me. "Do you like to sit here?" he asked me. "Sometimes," I said. "It's nice in the sun." "I put this bench here in memory of my son," he said. He patted the warm stone.)

At the end of the meadow the lilacs were in full bloom and the scent was overwhelming. We'd lived in Maine for a year when I was in nursery school, in a house with lilac bushes beside the porch. One of my first memories is of standing with my mother under one as she pulled a lilac blossom down to my nose. "Smell," she said. "Doesn't that smell good?" As I stood there, a bee buzzed and I saw a father pulling a stem down toward his toddler son, saying, "Smell," and the boy closed his eyes and breathed in. "Mmmm," he said. "That smells good."

My friend had been wrong. The festival was not for another week. But the trees on the Esplanade were already in bloom. People took pictures in elaborate groupings. The Esplanade is designed to draw your eyes down its majestic avenues of cherries, and so I'd never noticed the weeping cherry that stood off to the side. It was extremely tall, stretching upward with "weeps" that reached to the ground. I walked off the path, parted the blossoms, and stepped inside the circle of the tree's blooms.

Inside, there was a diffuse pink otherworldly light. By entering I had moved into another realm. I felt protected. In here I could detect my mother touching my skin. I thought: Stepping inside this "embrace" is the closest I am ever going to come to having my mother touch me in this world. Because my mother had loved these trees so much, she had poured something of herself into them, as if her soul had left her and entered them. Even if in no way did I think she was, literally, in the tree.

CHAPTER TEN

reckoning

On Friday of Memorial Day weekend, I drove out to visit a couple of friends in Montauk, a fishing town on the South Fork of Long Island. It was the first time I had been by the ocean since my mother's death. We strolled down the dock, past the boats. The air stank of salt and fish, like Cape Porpoise, the Maine town where we had lived when I was four and Liam was a toddler. Tired of the city, my parents wanted to live in the country. My father left his position at Saint Ann's and took a job on a boat as a commercial fisherman; my mother, who found part-time work making cakes for a local diner, would take us down to the harbor to meet the boat now and then. Sometimes my father would smuggle past the harbor police a lobster illegally caught in the nets, wrapping it in a sweater and throwing it to my mother. While we waited,

I liked to run along a series of paths on a cliff by the sea; they split and forked through the dune grass, heading off in mysterious directions, evoking all sorts of possible adventures. Now, in Montauk, when the reek of saltwater and fish hit me, a wave of understanding swelled: *My mother no longer exists.*

If children learn through exposure to new experiences, mourners *un*learn through exposure to absence in new contexts. Grief requires acquainting yourself with the world again and again; each "first" causes a break that must be reset. I knew, already, that the next time I visited the ocean, I would not be gutted like this. In this sense, my mother's death was not a single event, but a whole series of events—the first Easter without her; the first wedding anniversary without her; the first time Eamon, who has epilepsy, had a seizure and she was not here to calmly take charge. The lesson lay in the empty chair at the dinner table. It was learned night after night, day after day.

And so you always feel suspense, a queer dread—you never know what occasion will break the loss freshly open.

I spent all of Saturday on the beach. The waves were repetitive and rhythmic as memories. Liam and his friend J. came up to visit from Sag Harbor. We barbecued hamburgers on the deck, pouring fresh glasses of rosé till we got tipsy. There were Christmas lights over the fireplace, and in the soft light we played music and talked until we were exhausted. I went to bed buzzed and sun-flushed.

That night I dreamed of witnessing my mother's death

all over again. I woke gasping for breath, tears running down my face, with the jolt of relief all dreamers feel on waking: *Thank God. It was just a nightmare.*

Then came the realization that the nightmare was real. I had dreamed I'd watched my mother die.

I had, in fact, watched my mother die.

In the dream version, I was with my mother, my father, and my brothers in the ruined courtyard of an old hospital. Deep in a coma, my mother was strapped to a bulky steel contraption, part hospital bed, part electric chair. The pillared courtyard around her was crumbling. An orderly approached to tell us that a nurse would be putting my mother out of her misery in two minutes. "Your mother is scheduled to die at two-thirty," the orderly said.

I stood looking down at my mother, sick to my stomach.

I know you're going to die, I thought, *but I need you to say goodbye.*

But she was unresponsive.

Then, as the nurse approached with a cartoonishly large needle, my mother's left hand drifted through the hospital bed bars and gripped mine. Sand streamed off her hand. And I thought: *There is no fucking way I am going to stand here and watch my mother die. This is not to be borne.*

And I woke up.

Before my mother died I had never seen a dead body. My great-grandmother—my father's grandmother—died when I was in the fifth grade, but I didn't go to the funeral or the wake, because it would have meant missing school. My father went off alone, looking uncomfortable in a stiff black suit instead of his usual chamois shirts and jeans. I thought he looked like a figurine of himself. After that, death remained distant until one summer, after eighth grade, Finn, my dog, started to grow lethargic. He was eight years old, and I teased him when we jogged, yanking him along: Come on, old man. One day he wouldn't get up but lay panting on the floor of the cottage we'd rented in Cape Cod. The vet told us the news: Your dog has a large tumor in his heart, he said. We could operate, but we would have to cut open a flap in his chest—for some reason that phrase remains with me—and it would probably return anyway, so I would advise that you put him down.

I wanted to be the one to hold him. I sat on the cold linoleum floor of the office, in thin cotton shorts, and got Finn calm on my lap. They gave him a sedative and he yelped. Then came the needle as I petted him. He relaxed in my hands, the chemicals started their work, and I felt—felt—the life go out of him, drifting and then slamming, *gone*. For days I couldn't get that feeling out of my body. On the way home I didn't cry. But when I got to the house my mother looked at me and she was red-eyed. After dinner I went to bed so I could pull the blankets over my head and weep alone, the only way I ever could, and in the dark came footsteps and my mother at the edge of the bed said, "It's sad, Meg, I'm sad too," and stroked my shoulder.

I didn't feel better. But I remember that she tried.

When I was a freshman in college, the thirty-three-year-old daughter of one of my parents' friends died suddenly. I remember coming home over Thanksgiving break and finding my mom deeply upset. At the time we had a habit of giving each other the new Dick Francis mystery for Christmas. She took me out to buy a winter coat and as we walked down Fourteenth Street, she told me how shaken she was by Liza's death. Then she suddenly said, "I have a present for you," and pulled out of her bag the new Dick Francis mystery, a big yellow hardback.

"But it's not Christmas."

"I know," she said. "Liza's death made me feel anything can happen. Something terrible could happen tomorrow. I want you to have this now. Why do we wait for holidays to give gifts?" Her voice was shaky, and it was the first time as an adult that I really felt that one day she would be gone.

The day after the dream, I woke with my lungs burning. It was difficult to breathe. I couldn't help thinking that my dream and my condition were related.

I had just been reading a passage in Darian Leader's *The New Black* about "killing the dead"—the theory that a mourner has to make a choice between holding on to her grief and moving forward by killing the dead. The fact that we feel both affection and hostility toward the ones we love complicates mourning. Most people don't know how to be angry at the dead. It seems ignoble and perhaps beside the point to speak (or think) ill of them. And so, Leader notes, bereaved people often "become angry with colleagues, friends, and lovers without linking this displacement consciously to their loss," while idealizing their relationships with those who have died. To "kill the dead" metaphorically is a way "of loosening one's bonds to them," Leader observes, and in fact many mourners do dream about murdering or witnessing the murder of the person they have lost.

Certainly, I'd been angry at my mother for not—in the word I kept returning to—"supporting" my divorce. But now that she was gone, I did not want to kill her; I was not ready to loosen the bonds. Kill the dead? No, no, no. I did not want my mother dead. I felt the same insistence that the child feels in *Green Eggs and Ham*. I do not like green eggs and ham; I do not like them, Sam I am. I will not eat them in the rain, etc. *I do not want my mother dead. I will not accept it in my head.* But was this partly because I was refusing to accept her in all her complexity, because I was idealizing her? Over the next days, my chest got tighter. I developed an itch in my throat, which became a dry, insistent cough, making it hard to breathe deeply. It didn't occur to me to go the doctor, and I went to work, where I was wrapping things up before leaving. But I experienced an apathy nearly as intense as the one I experienced right after my mother's death. I couldn't focus, and whenever I slept I dreamed of her.

I thought of what the painter Dora Carrington wrote in her journal after her beloved, the writer and critic Lytton Strachey, died in 1932:

I dreamt of you again last night. And when I woke up it was as if you had died afresh. Every day I find it *harder* to bear. For what point is there in life now? . . . I look at our favorites, I try and read them, but without you they give me no pleasure. . . . It is impossible to think that I shall never sit with you again and hear your laugh. *That every day for the rest of my life you will be away.*

Carrington killed herself a few weeks afterward. I had not lost my spouse; it was my father who had. But like Carrington, I was experiencing the loss of a home—even if it was more a remembered than an actual home. My divorce intensified my sense of dislocation. *I have no home,* I would think self-pityingly to myself when I was unable to sleep.

I didn't go to the doctor because I wanted my mother to come back.

If I did not take care of myself, I imagined, she would have to.

One night, I went to a movie at a multiplex in Chelsea after going to see my therapist, who heard my cough and told me to go to the doctor. My throat began to itch as I sat in the theater. I coughed until I thought I might pass out. I gathered my things, but, growing light-headed in the foyer, I sat in one of the leather chairs strewn about and laid my head back. As I did, I thought, *I might die here.* I thought it semi-facetiously, the way one does when fending off a fear.

Then I had a pang: *What if my lungs were filling with fluid and I* was *going to die here, in the upper lobby of the Chelsea movie theater?*

I stood up and got myself through the rain to the subway. When I got home, I called my doctor for antibiotics. My mother wasn't coming back, and if I kept hoping she would, I might end up with pneumonia.

When I woke the next day, I was flooded by the physicality of my body and my mind. *How odd that this body is going to wear out!* I thought. Then: *One day this body is going to wear out.* I lay back in the sheets and enjoyed the sensation of cotton, of morning, of my body, even of the chest muscles sore from coughing. Death and the sun are not to be looked at steadily, La Rochefoucauld wrote. Mother, I am confronting yours, here, as I write. But I have not come to terms with my own.

The idea of self-extinction is terrifying to most of us. "There is no death, there is only me—me who is going to die," wrote André Malraux. It makes my stomach turn thinking about it. The dread of death is so primal, it overtakes me on a molecular level. In the lowest moments, it produces nihilism. If I am going to die, why not get it over with? Why live in this agony of anticipation?

I first understood death when I was eight. It was the summer. School had just gotten out and the warm June air was rich with anticipation. Soon we would be in Vermont, and I would do nothing but read, swim, and eat corn and ice cream. A few days before we left, my friend Katie came over for the afternoon. She and my brother and I played freeze tag in the apartment. She was "it," and she trapped me behind the dining room table. I called out to my brother to come get me. Frozen, I put my hand down on its edge and idly fitted my finger into the narrow groove that connected the oak table leaves to a border of lighter wood. As I did, a shock struck me, like cold lightning. It ran up and down my body and grounded me to the linoleum.

I am going to die, I realized.

I would die, and I wouldn't see my mother or my father or my dogs or my house when that happened. I would simply . . . not exist. This had never occurred to me before.

And my mother and father were going to die! Before I did, most likely. This was not what I had been promised. I had been promised sun and summer and green trees and water and books and then cooling air and fall and wind and chill and snow and Christmas lights and New Year's slush and ice and then balminess and rain and the green buds of trees and summer all over. Not this gift of life and then, abruptly, an *end.*

I waited in a panic for my brother to unfreeze me—and in a mess of hurtling kinetic energy, he did, bumping into me, squealing, running away. And I ran to my mother, who was trying to read while we played, and hugged her and tried to crawl into her lap, a rare act, which she met with both bemusement and annoyance, saying, "Go on, it's rude not to be a good host," and pushed me away. Then, noting some sadness in my eyes, she kissed the back of my hand.

All that summer, death haunted me. Before, I'd liked to

stay up late to read after my parents put me to bed. I pretended to be scared of the dark, and they would leave the hall light on; I could read by angling my book toward the door. Now, though, I lay in bed, wracked by thoughts of extinction. The idea that I wouldn't exist terrified me. I imagined it as being buried alive, a senselessness that could nonetheless be felt. How could my parents have brought me into a world that would only be snatched from me? Yet they had. Better, it seemed, never to have been born.

On these nights, I would listen to the traffic swooshing by outside, wrapped in my quilt, and work myself into a state of horror so profound that I would become nauseated and run to the bathroom to throw up. It continued into the fall. "What's wrong?" my mother would say, emerging from the dining room where she'd been sitting with my father, wineglass in hand. "I feel sick to my stomach," I said.

I had a terror that my parents would die in an accident. They often went out with friends after work and if they were late—as they always were—my heart would begin to pound. *Where are you?* I would ask when they called. *Don't worry, we're coming,* they'd say breezily, bar glasses clinking in the background.

When I went back to school, I looked around at my classmates, wondering if they had experienced a similar terror during summer break. At Hwa Yuan, a Chinese restaurant my family went to nearly every Friday night, I gazed at all the well-dressed professionals and felt sick, as if I were looking at corpses rotting around me. "I have to throw up,"

I blurted, and hurtled down the narrow stairs of the restaurant to the disgusting, undersized toilet, and retched. I couldn't make anything come up.

When I got upstairs, I looked around and told myself, *I am younger than everyone else here, and they are managing to eat and enjoy themselves. So I have to just assume I am going to live a long life. And I will bookmark this fear for later. I can worry about it when I'm forty or fifty.* And gradually my fear abated.

One night, the old dread returned. My parents came home to find me awake and in tears. As my father walked the babysitter home, my mother took me on her lap, her perfume (Shalimar) and her hair enveloping me, and she, too, began to cry.

"Why are you crying?" I asked through my tears.

"Sometimes even grown-ups cry, Meg," she said. "Sometimes grown-ups are sad too."

Why was she sad that night? It is lost now. My mother was two years younger than I am today.

I WAS unable to push these questions aside: What are we to do with the knowledge that we die? What bargain do you make in your mind so as not to go crazy with fear of the predicament, a predicament none of us knowingly chose to enter? You can believe in God and heaven, if you have the capacity for faith. Or, if you don't, you can do what a stoic like Seneca did, and push away the awfulness by noting that if death is indeed extinction, it won't hurt, for we won't experience it. "It would be dreadful could it remain with you; but of necessity either it does not arrive or else it departs," he wrote.

If this logic fails to comfort, you can decide, as Plato and Jonathan Swift did, that since death is natural, and the gods must exist, it cannot be a bad thing. As Swift said, "It is impossible that anything so natural, so necessary, and so universal as death, should ever have been designed by Providence as an evil to mankind." And Socrates: "I am quite ready to admit . . . that I ought to be grieved at death, if I were not persuaded in the first place that I am going to other gods who are wise and good." But this is poor comfort to those of us who have no gods to turn to. If you love this world, how can you look forward to departing it? Rousseau wrote, "He who pretends to look on death without fear lies. All men are afraid of dying, this is the great law of sentient beings, without which the entire human species would soon be destroyed." Philip Larkin puts it even more directly, calling the fear of death the "special way of being afraid / No trick dispels":

> . . . Religion used to try,
> That vast moth-eaten musical brocade
> Created to pretend we never die,
> And specious stuff that says No rational being
> Can fear a thing it cannot feel, not seeing
> That this is what we fear—no sight, no sound,

No touch or taste or smell, nothing to think with,
Nothing to love or link with,
The anesthetic from which none come round.

And yet without death our lives would lose their shape: "Death is the mother of beauty," Wallace Stevens wrote. Or as a character in Don DeLillo's *White Noise* says, "I think it's a mistake to lose one's sense of death, even one's fear of death. Isn't death the boundary we need?" It's not clear that DeLillo means us to agree, but I think I do. I love the world more because it is transient.

Studies have shown that faith helps Americans fear death less. But believing in heaven doesn't protect you from the intensities of grief. To contemplate death in any serious way, even as a believer, is to wonder what change death wreaks upon us. In the occasional moments when I believe in forces we cannot see, I still find it impossible to believe in the cinematic image of loved ones waiting for me just like normal—if slightly diaphanous and shimmering—as I cross a river into their yearning embrace. It simply does not make sense that so enormous a transition would lead to so similar an existence.

And even if death doesn't lead to extinction, it still means that, in the best of circumstances, one will never see one's loved one again in this form—never be able to share jokes, hug, have a glass of wine. I don't just miss my mother's soul, after all. I miss her laugh, her sarcasm, and the sound of her voice saying my name. I miss her hands, which I shall never see again, for we have burned her body into fine, charcoal ash and small white bones, and that is what is now left of her voice and her eyes and her fingernails. That loss is not recuperable, regardless of what one believes about the afterlife. That's what, I think, C. S. Lewis, a practicing Christian, was wrestling with when he wrote this about the death of his wife:

> Suppose that the earthly lives she and I shared for a few years are in reality only the . . . earthly appearance of two unimaginable, supercosmic, eternal somethings. . . . Two circles that touched. But those two circles, above all the point at which they touched, are the very thing I am mourning for, homesick for, famished for. You tell me, 'she goes on.' But my heart and body are crying out, come back, come back. Be a circle, touching my circle on the plane of Nature. But I know this is impossible. I know that the thing I want is exactly the thing I can never get. The old life, the jokes, the drinks, the arguments, the lovemaking, the tiny, heartbreaking commonplace.

If one doesn't believe in an afterlife, then one is faced with letting go—really and truly letting go—of the hope of ever seeing your beloved again. I for one had not been able to truly accept that I would never see my mother again, except in the mad, three a.m. moments when I woke with a start, the apprehension settling around me: She is dead—*dead*—and I too will be dead.

One would think that living so proximately to the provisional would ruin life, and at times it did make it hard. But at other times I experienced the world with less fear and more clarity. It didn't matter if I was in line for an extra two minutes. I could take in the sensations of color, sound, life. How strange that we should live on this planet and make cereal boxes, and shopping carts, and gum! That we should renovate stately old banks and replace them with Trader Joe's! We were ants in a sugar bowl, and one day the bowl would empty.

O UR ANXIETY about death is so powerful that it seems hard to believe that it isn't timeless and universal. But as Philippe Ariès shows in *The Hour of Our Death*, a history of how Western culture views death, people in the past thought differently about what death was and how it should be dealt with. It's not that people ever greeted the death of their loved ones with indifference: mourning seems to be a permanent part of the human condition. (And not just the human condition; elephants and chimpanzees mourn, too.) But in the medieval period, Ariès shows, death in the West was "tame," that is, it seemed "close and familiar" rather than terrifying. The tame death could exist because the "distance between life and death was not traditionally perceived as a 'radical metamorphosis.'" The dead were thought to be sleepers awaiting a future resurrection (hence the phrase "Rest in peace"). Death was part of everyday life, and individuals prepared for it calmly, with the aid of family and community, making themselves right with God. Over time, the rise of individualism made people more attached to this world, and therefore more anxious about their own mortality. But even in the eighteenth and nineteenth centuries, death was not yet seen as something to be looked away from: indeed, for the Romantics, death was "beautiful," carrying with it an exalted narcotic sweetness, something to be longed for as well as feared.

Ariès suggests, though, that the cult of the beautiful death was in part the product of a rising anxiety about death. In the twentieth century, that anxiety—the one most of us live with every day—grew so pronounced that death was silenced. For most of us, death is an absolute break: a form of extinction too painful to consider. And so, Ariès says, we look away from it, pretending we might vanquish it one day through better nutrition and superior medical care. Where earlier cultures thought it crucial to contemplate death—"it is of the utmost importance for mortals to listen to the lessons of the dead," wrote the Abbé Porée in the eighteenth century—we push it aside.

Tolstoy's *The Death of Ivan Ilyich*, written in 1886, captures this shift. The book opens with the announcement that Ivan Ilyich has died. His colleague Pyotr Ivanovich visits Ilyich's wife. "Surely he wasn't conscious?" Pyotr Ivanovich asks. " 'He was,' she whispered, 'until the last moment.' " Pyotr

Ivanovich is horrified at the thought of "the suffering of a man he had known so well":

> "It might begin right now, at any minute, for me too," he thought, and for a moment he became afraid. But immediately, how he did not know himself, the usual thought came to his aid that it had happened to Ivan Ilyich, and not to him, and that it should not and could not happen to him.

This passage may be the first modern description of the psychological process, familiar to us all, of silencing our fear and distancing ourselves through repression.

Ivan Ilyich's death is also "silent"—and modern—in another sense: everyone knows he is dying and no one will acknowledge it. They treat him like a child, infantilizing him. This repression makes him angry:

> Ivan Ilyich's chief torment was the lie—the lie that was for some reason acknowledged by all—that he was only ill and was not dying, and that he only needed to keep calm and undergo treatment, and that something very good would come of it.

In the past, ministering to the dying was an important, even cherished part of life. But attitudes toward caretaking, too, have shifted. As the extended family fell apart—and as dying became something to be silenced rather than something holy and even transcendent—people began to fear that their deaths might be "burdensome." One of the most upsetting facts I've come across since my mother's death was in a 2004 survey about end-of-life attitudes among Nebraskans. In the section titled "Very Important Aspects of Dealing with or Thinking About Dying," "not being a burden" was a concern of eighty-three percent of those surveyed. Our squeamishness about death has impoverished the way we die, it would seem. The ill body gives the lie to our repression of death; it exposes the lie that medicine will offer a *solution* to the body, dissolving it, one happy day, into pure spirit, or allowing us to survive as a brain in a jar.

I KEPT REMEMBERING days I'd forgotten. One summer, when I was eight, my father took Liam and me fishing on Moosehead Lake in Maine, where we went canoe camping sometimes. It was a hazy and hot day. We had practiced casting on the shore. I asked my father why he fly-fished instead of using a regular rod like ours and he said it was because flies didn't hurt the fish. You could catch a fish with a fly and throw it back. I liked to study the flies in his kit with their bright green threads. They were almost toys. But the barb on the end of our lines would likely go through the fish's throat and kill it one way or another.

By the time we got in the canoe and paddled out, the lake was getting flat and the sun was low in the sky by the bluish pines. We were going where the fish were, and I was wondering how I could have let this happen. I didn't want to fish. I had wanted to do it only because it was what my father did. But he fished in a way that didn't hurt the fish. I trailed my hand in the water and let the brown and green plants slide past. The sky was bright. Liam was excited but I was quiet and for once didn't care to compete. "What's wrong, Meg? Do you need help?" my father said. No, I said, and told them I was going to watch. I sat quietly. I was ashamed for wanting something without understanding what wanting it meant. I sat quietly and looked at the nesting loons, eager to get back to shore.

As I've mourned, I have been surprised by how few people asked what to me is the most pressing question of all: Where do you think the dead go? What happens to the dead? Over fifteen months only two people, both of them men I had just met, asked me this question. In the past, it would have been clear to each of us what the other believed. But in this world we may not know what our peers and friends think about this most pressing of questions. Many nonreligious people, I've found, believe that there is some kind of after-existence. Some religious people make it clear that they don't know what to believe the afterlife will be like. A "transcendental, psychedelic trip," one of the men, a regular churchgoer with a penchant for drugs, said he was hoping it might be. Even the spiritually minded are uncertain about the contours of life after death. And most of us remain attached to the pleasures of *this* world: the calling of the loons at dusk, the soothing wind over a lake.

CHAPTER ELEVEN

reevaluation

In July, I went to Paris to give a poetry reading. I spent the first two days in a jet-lagged daze, afraid to leave my hotel. The room was dirty and cold, and ants congregated around the minibar. I closed the curtains and slept through the morning and afternoon. I woke, exhausted. I was supposed to read in two hours. I felt leaden. I have no idea how to continue, I thought, in bewilderment. It will never get better. "I'm not mourning. I'm suffering," the French theorist Roland Barthes wrote after his mother died. Yet I was ashamed of my pain; it seemed abnormal.

When I'd been in the airport, waiting for my plane, my friend Vanessa had called me. "You've been handling this with grace," she said, kindly. "You deserve to have some fun."

Now I was stupid with anger at myself for thinking I was handling anything well. It just meant I was hiding everything.

I walked up the rue des Saints-Pères and went to Café de Flore to order a hard-boiled egg and a café crème. The waiter asked if I liked croissants. Yes, I said, uncertainly. He brought two croissants. I looked at them. They looked like alien maggots. I drank the café crème, spooning sugar in. It was sweet and comforting. Finally I got in a taxi and went to the reading. The building was locked, and I couldn't figure out how to get in. I began to panic, tears rising to my eyes. Finally, two men approached and pressed a buzzer I hadn't seen, and the door opened; I followed them, chagrined at my lack of inner resources. The rest of the world had its feet on the ground. I didn't even notice the buttons you were supposed to press. *Just press the buttons,* I told myself.

That night, I slept quietly for the first time since arriving. The next day, I made myself get up early and go to the Musée d'Orsay.

The only other time I'd visited Paris I had been with my mother, who'd been chaperoning a school trip. Fresh out of college, I tagged along. We shared a hotel room. I remember being disturbed by our proximity. Paris was the home of the exiles—where writers went to be writers, wild and narcotic and alone. Instead, here I lay, listening to my mother breathe asthmatically.

My most vivid memory was our visit to the Musée d'Orsay, where she marveled at Monet's *The Magpie*, which neither of us had ever seen. The painting depicts a snowy field by a barn and a single magpie in the midst of the barren stillness. Monet painted relatively few snowscapes. He was more interested in the summer's wildly various light than in the equalizing neutrality of winter's. The tones of *The Magpie* are cool and monotonous—whites, browns, grays, yellows. But to the left, the eye notices a startling dab of black and focuses to see a magpie sitting on the fence. The bird is the only black in the painting. It is unusual; most paintings, if you look closely, rely heavily on black for shadows and depth. The landscape organizes itself around this dab, once you've noticed it.

My mother was fascinated. "Do you see how there is no black?" she said to me.

"I do," I said.

"It changes everything," she said. "It is amazing to me how such a simple thing could change everything."

And we were very happy standing there.

The mourner's mind is superstitious, looking for signs and wonders. At the museum once again, I secretly felt that if I found *The Magpie*, my mother would be resurrected beside me to look at it once more, like a *Star Wars* hologram recording you could play over and over. But the physical space did not cooperate: the paintings were hung on different walls, in different rooms, and I couldn't find it. Tired, I started for the exit. Looking at the floor map, I saw I'd missed a room holding paintings by Manet and Monet on the first floor. I climbed past the sculptures toward the room. And there it was.

In a spring landscape, you might never notice the magpie, but in this wintry image it stands out. There is an exaggerated sense of solitude; the bird is the only sign of life in all the stillness. Most Impressionist landscapes were painted *"en plein air,"* with an emphasis on capturing the moment in which they were made. But the art historian Charles S. Moffett points out that *The Magpie* couldn't have been painted entirely this way. It is a painting from memory, even though it appears to capture a specific moment: the shadows striking the snow just so. The painting summoned absence—and yet as a piece of art it was entirely present. There was something witchy about it. My mother was that winter light, it occurred to me—reconstituted only in memory. And the little bird on the gate, perched in quietude, what was that? I suppose you could see it as hope: a sign of continuity. Later I discovered that the gift shop sells more postcards of *The Magpie* than of any other painting in the museum. People flock to *Starry Night*, but they take *The Magpie* home with them. Months afterward, I went into my mother's office—left mainly as she'd had it—to find some batteries. There, on the shelf to the left, were her books—*A Guide to Great Gingerbread*; *Yoga and You*—and photos of her dancing with my brothers. In the middle stood a postcard of *The Magpie*. I hadn't even known. She had it, I said, right by her desk.

. . .

On my last Sunday in Paris, I went to Notre Dame and lit a votive candle for my mother, then sat as they began the Vespers service. *I know you would hate this,* I whispered to her. *But I don't know what else to do. I want to remember you. And the last time I was here we came here together. And you marveled at the height of the ceiling and the beauty of stained glass. You wanted to look at old things before you died and this is old.*

The bells rang for Vespers, and I listened to the music, tears running down my face.

When I returned to my hotel a light rain was falling. I was restless so I went back out, murmuring to the concierge, "Be back soon," as if he were my father, then wandered past the gay bars to an old gelato place as the rain fell on me.

I thought I was prepared for my mother's death.

I knew it would happen.

Yet the reality of her *being dead* was so different from her death.

I WENT to New Hampshire for four weeks that reminded me of my childhood summers. I read and wrote all day, swam in the afternoons, and spent the nights eating and talking late into the dark. For the first sustained period, I felt my old self plump up and the shadows shrink.

Then my father called me on a Friday night in July, as I

was studying the way the setting sun had turned the clouds pink against the light-blue sky. He sounded distraught. "Meg, I wanted to tell you that Ringo isn't doing so well," he said. "He's standing around, panting, and I can't get him to eat much. And I have to go to this wedding tomorrow, and I have never done something like that without your mother. She was always the one who could get me out the door."

I told him that he should do whatever felt comfortable, that everyone would understand. He exhaled and said, "I'm just worried about Ringo. I was talking to Eamon, and he said it seems that Ringo has changed an enormous amount since Mom died. It's true. Some nights I go outside and Ringo is standing on the driveway, just standing there, looking out, like he is waiting for someone, searching for them."

There was not much I could say to comfort him. I had the distinct sense that Ringo was going to die soon. When I had stopped at my dad's on my way to New Hampshire, I'd seen Ringo and thought: *It's going to happen any day.* Diana and I had been throwing balls for Ringo and her dog, Ajax, and he came trotting back to us at an odd angle. "He looks like a drunken sailor!" Diana laughed.

Ringo had been a present for Eamon when he was a boy. But my mother was the real animal lover in our family. She had wanted to be a vet when she was young. She'd always been the one to feed our dogs and groom them and train them. She took Ringo to obedience classes; sweet-tempered by nature, he became the gentlest dog I'd ever spent time with. He was afraid of small spaces under furniture. My mother used to love to watch him look at a ball under a chair and whine.

You big baby, she would say. You big baby. What are you doing? Get it. Get the ball!

And sometimes, after standing there for minutes looking at the tennis ball, he would. Then he would look up at her as if he was proud.

"Anyway, I got a different kind of food," my dad said, "and when I gave it to him, he ate it quickly, like he was starving. I just have to pay attention. Ringo is going on twelve. Big dogs get sick when they get that old. But it makes you feel that you are up against the inevitability of things. After what we went through this winter, it makes you feel you are up against the inevitability of things."

His voice broke. "I have this crazy feeling of 'What can I do?' Because I went through this before, and the outcome was one I was not happy with. I did what I could, everything I could, and the outcome was really not an outcome I'm happy with."

He paused. I heard him breathe in.

"When are the gods going to stop?"

Two days later he called back.

"I had to put Ringo to sleep," he said. His voice was hoarse.

He'd taken the dog to the vet for a set of tests, and one came back showing that Ringo had a tumor in his chest. "They could have operated, but he would have been in extreme discomfort and pain afterward," my father said. He was almost in tears. "I couldn't put him through more."

At first I thought Ringo represented my mother to my father, and that in Ringo's sickness my father was reliving my mother's—finding better food, adjusting medicines. But now it seemed to me that *he* identified with Ringo. We were all talking about ourselves. *We* are ailing. We lurch like drunken sailors even when we come together for a birthday or a holiday.

Y OU REMEMBER her in flashes. The flashes hurt. They light up your stomach. Then you breathe, look out again.

At a party, you say *my dead mother.* You explain, *She died at Christmas.*

Christmas? Ohh . . . comes the pitying response.
Yes.

It hurts. Then you explain: *But it's good. We can all be together if we want to. We will never forget this is the day our mother died.*

You are learning the narrative. You are establishing the catechism, responses to the questions:

A: *She was sick for two years.*
A: *Yes, cancer.*
A: *She died on Christmas Day.*
A: *We were all with her.*
A: *She was young—I mean, she was relatively young, fifty-five.*
A: *She was a teacher and then an administrator.*
A: *She grew up in New Jersey.*
A: *My father is OK.*
A: *My brothers are doing OK. [Pause] It is very hard for all of us.*
A: *No, that's OK.*

And you are thinking in some chamber inside your heart: *Fuck, fuck, fuck. How dare you turn pain to reason?*

In those moments I *want* to hurt, like an outraged child in a sulk. But quickly a day passes and I've enjoyed myself in the sun, or at dinner, having a glass of wine, talking to friends, reading, talking, not thinking about death.

Yesterday, while I was brushing my teeth, I raised my face to the mirror and unexpectedly saw myself. And I thought: I am becoming someone whose mother is dead.

Then a cool sadness flooded me. It was true. I was getting used to her being dead. My mother was gone. And I: letting her go.

Then, one morning in New Hampshire, I see a river moving lazily in the sun and I start to cry, because the water is moving so fast. I am doing laundry with two older women and they talk about how hard it is to buy gifts for your mother and I get a lump in my throat and excuse myself to get detergent. I am always wanting either to hide away or to plunge into a "systematic derangement of the senses," as Rimbaud would have it. I drive too fast. When running, I cross the street in front of cars. With other people, with strangers, I count the hours until I can go be alone and get back to my secret preoccupation, my romance with my lost mother. This is what I need to do, remember her, puzzle over her, understand the difference between us. I trust that one day I'll stop needing to do this.

One night I am lying in bed in my room in a creaky

old house. It is a warm summer night. Mosquitoes buzz around me. The light is on, I have been reading *Remembrance of Things Past*, I nod off and wake up. I have a profound, spreading sense that I have been here in this room before. I have felt this pain before. I have seen this very light, I have felt this very temperature, I have known this very feeling of loneliness—except this time I know it is part of the pattern, I am at one with the universe, everything is interconnected. I feel an extreme peace. I am OK. My mother is there. I am in a vision of the universe I love. Nothing need be disturbed, and I could—perhaps I should—die now and all would be well. It is like a waking dream and for a second I have the distinct sense of a voice telling me this is right, it is the moment, I *could* die, all is well, and this is the moment to end on. The "world" seems very far away. Furniture and its edges; light; all seems in retreat, disposable.

A F T E R   A   L O S S, you have to learn to believe the dead one is dead. It doesn't come naturally. One July day, I went for a swim in Willard Pond, now an Audubon preserve, where there is a family of nesting loons. I'd spent time reading in the sun, and my arms were getting brown. I had gained weight in the months after my mother died—I kept eating ice cream and cereal late at night when I missed her—but for once I wasn't totally unhappy about the feeling of extra flesh, detecting in the weight a comforting, maternal presence, as if I were mothering my own body.

She would like this pond, I thought. So today I'll go there for her. Driving out, because driving was still so new to me, I imagined who she was when she was thirty-three, what the experience of those summers in Vermont was like for her. I realized she would have had two kids in tow (my brother and me) and was about to become pregnant with her third. I would have been ten. She would, on an afternoon like today, have been driving us down to the covered bridge to swim. I wondered if perhaps she sometimes felt shy, exploring new places with two children and no other adults around—a question I'd never asked myself before. It was because I felt shy going by myself to swim. And then I thought, having children means you have a clear reason for being wherever you are in the summer—at the beach, at the store. There we would be, tugging at her hands, saying, "Mom, Mom—did you see? There was a frog on that rock." And she would tease and say, "A frog? No, you didn't see a frog." And we would point and she would pretend not to see and then she would dive into the freezing water, and swim against the current, goofing around with us.

I went to the pond for her. Diving in, I felt for a moment that I *was* my mother. But I was aware that she was dead; I could feel it in the shadows in the green leaves. *This is where the dead live,* I thought, *in the holes in the leaves where the insects are biting through.*

One warm day I went running. I passed a field where horses shuddered in the heat, flicking flies with their ears, and sheep were lying down and grazing at the same time, a vision of laziness. The trees rustled in the breeze, black and green, steeped in sun; there was a lazy buzz of airplanes far overhead. The sheepdog was stretched out on the crest of the hill in repose, a ball of white fluff in the shimmer of the hazy sun. Two nights earlier, after a hard day, I'd had a dream in which my mother held up a ladybug in spectral, gray fingers and said: "When you feel heartsick, just remember this: You are really *eye*sick. You are not looking at things closely enough."

As I looked, everything moved, jingling slightly against everything else; the world, quietly, brightly alive.

A MONTH after Ringo died, my father called. I'd driven back to New York, where it was muggy, and I'd opened the window and was leaning out the fire escape, watching people across our backyards move around in front of their TVs, making dinner.

"The Perseid meteor showers are here," he told me. "And I've been eating dinner outside and then lying in the lounge chairs watching the stars like your mother and I used to"—at some point he stopped calling her Mom—"and that helps. It might sound strange, but I was sitting there, looking up at the sky, and I thought, 'You are but a mote of dust. And your troubles and travails are just a mote of a mote of dust.' And it helped me. I have allowed myself to think about things I had been scared to think about and feel. And it allowed me to be there—to be present. Whatever my life is, whatever my loss is, it's small in the face of all that existence.

"Last night Uncle Stephen and Aunt Barbara came over for dinner," he continued. "A few months ago a night like this would make me feel bad the next day; it was so obvious your mother wasn't there. But not this time. The meteor shower changed something. I was looking the other way through a telescope before: I was just looking at what was not there. Now I look at what is there."

I knew that death terrified him, and I imagined that my mother's death terrified him about his own death, though he made only oblique references to it, talking about how "one doesn't want to be forgotten." Sometimes when we were all together at dinner he sat quietly as we blathered about the latest movie and shouted over one another boisterously, and he picked at the food on his plate, bags drooping under his eyes, and I felt sorry that we were not making more effort to say, *Dad, Dad, we are not forgetting you.* But we're not used to talking this way.

ONE OF THE MOST confusing manifestations of grief was a flickering on-and-off relationship to sex. At many points after my mother's death I felt a slight aversion to it. It seemed exhausting, all that touching. What was wrong with me? I wondered. After M. had disappeared, something in me got locked away, and for a while I reverted to a distanced, frozen place. Part of me felt terror at the prospect of intimacy. And yet part of me was compelled to seek it out. I drifted into disconnected encounters and relationships I had no business being in. There was something experimental about the way I did this, a conviction that nothing mattered very much—although maybe I was also hoping to find out, through sex, that this conviction might be false. In all of these encounters it was as if I stood on a high plain and a black wind whipped through me, a wind of need; I had the feeling that I was falling down a rabbit hole to Wonderland. Or rather—I was already in Wonderland and, come hell or high water, these would be my companions. I threw myself into a man's life, eager to get beneath whatever mask he wore, even when I felt nothing specific toward *him*. I was absorbed in the cathartic contact that would end, once again, with my own spreading sense of loneliness. It may be that what I really wanted was to find a way to reenact that loneliness, and I got it each time I closed the door on someone. Or perhaps I wanted, cruelly, for them to feel the pain I felt. Whatever the case, at all times, I had an intensified—intoxicated— sense of my own aloneness. Mostly I was pretending. I was capable of being convincing, since I was already role-playing all the time. And then one day I would wake up to the falseness of my own storytelling, and walk away.

This was careless of me, I now know, but I was not capable of taking care. Because I had few barriers—I felt I had no skin—it must have seemed as if I was open, confiding, needing to reveal myself, and this quality seemed to draw others in. But my primary romance was with my dead mother. And when, after I moved on, a few of them got angry with me, it surprised me: Didn't they understand that their pain was small and manageable, nothing compared with losing your mother to illness and oblivion? I hadn't meant to spread pain, but I had.

In August, a man I dated after my mother's death texted me about how important it was "not to avoid." I told him I wasn't avoiding him; I just had other things going on. I needed to see my father and my brothers; that was my priority. When he talked about the importance of not avoiding things I wanted to laugh bleakly, because every nerve in my body still hurt from everything I *hadn't* avoided; arrogantly, I thought that whatever his need, it was nothing in the scheme of loss that I had endured. And I didn't want to take responsibility for it—that was the ugly truth. Over and over I found myself resenting anyone who tried to impose his feelings, his demands, on me; couldn't he see it was all I could do to keep myself moving forward, that whatever energy I had left had to be devoted to my family? A person who did come to see this was Jim. One day when we were talking on the phone, I suddenly said, "I have to go," and hung up. When we spoke the next day, he said, "It's OK. I get it. You just don't want to be accountable to anyone else." It was true; but that was because I felt I *couldn't* be.

For all the solicitude in the world, it would be impossible for anyone else to understand what I had gone through and how depleted it had left me. When a man I'd dated asked me to recommend a book that would help him understand "this whole grief thing" I found myself shaking with anger. My mother died, I thought, it's not a "thing." Every piece of fury I'd carried in my body over the past year was now irrationally directed at him. He *couldn't* understand. He had not made a home with a husband and then disassembled it while his mother was slowly killed by metastasizing cells. But— but—it was not his fault my mother died, I thought, calming myself. And it was not the fault of my friends, whom I still sometimes snapped at when they reassured me that one day I'd feel better. I didn't get to punish them just because I wanted to smash a stick over someone's head. This man had been kind to me; what he didn't understand wasn't a crime. I was ornery and judgmental, ready to pick a cosmic fight over scraps. Sometimes, loss seemed to have enlarged me; at other times, it shrank me to this position of wounded, baffled anger.

CHAPTER TWELVE

abundance/abandonment

In August, my friend C., an artist, called me with a proposition. He told me if I was in mourning, I should visit Detroit. It was a strange thing to say but I liked it; it gently reminded me how small my grief was without diminishing its reality. On arriving, I shivered to see how desolate the city was. Entire blocks were given over to abandoned parking lots and buildings. There is no center, no comforting "good neighborhood," the way there is in New Orleans or Chicago. Instead, even the "best" blocks are studded with abandoned buildings and open concrete lots. The mood oscillates from building to building. The whole city is in grief.

On a cool late-summer day, C. and I drove out to Corktown, the oldest surviving neighborhood in Detroit. "I want to show you something," he said, wheeling the car to the left. "This is going to blow your mind."

"What?"

"Can't you guess?" He nodded his head to the side of the road. I saw a looming structure behind the commercial buildings. "Your mind is going to be so blown. It is going to be in little pieces everywhere."

"The train station," I said.

He had told me about the abandoned train station. He is from Zimbabwe, and his accent turns the word "abandoned" into the word "abundant." I misheard him the first time he'd mentioned it. No, he said, *a-ban-doned*.

The building is a majestic example of Beaux-Arts architecture. At the base you see the grand arches typical of train stations built in the early twentieth century. Above it rise ornate upper floors that used to hold offices. Implacably, it looms over the landscape, and yet every window is broken, the arches boarded, barbed wire surrounding it, a reminder of doom and glory at once. It's a temple of confidence—architectural confidence, civic confidence, urban confidence—in gap-toothed decay, at once monstrous and magnificent. As we looked at it, a couple of German tourists pulled up to take photos.

The train station took me back to something I had read in Harrison's *The Dominion of the Dead*. Ruins remind us that mortal time is only one kind of time, because, in their transitional state, they dramatize death. They embody what we know to be true only abstractly: that we and the things we make decay, and our whole history is a dot in time. As John Updike once put it, generally "disappearance has no appearance." Ruins also represent an idea of a future that has not come to pass, an alternate universe in which things didn't happen this way— one of the mourner's preoccupations.

The decline of a city is not the same as the death of a human. But the visual decay of Detroit resonated with me. In the midst of all that emptiness reverberated what I could think of only as a desolate resilience. People were taking advantage of government stimulus money to buy homes, and artists and farmers were repurposing old buildings. And in the midst of all the urban ruin, green trees were everywhere. I asked C. about them.

"Those are called 'ghetto palms' because they grow in neglected corners of the city," he said. "Owners hate them: Their roots grow so deep and so fast they crack the foundations of buildings."

At C.'s apartment, I read more about the ghetto palm in one of his books. The tree was imported to California during the nineteenth-century gold rush by a wave of Chinese immigrants, who treasured it for its medicinal properties. But it took to the soil and climate all too well and now it grows all over. It can grow pretty much anywhere because its roots are deep and because it has long wide leaves that scoop up water. It also smells bad, so it stinks up the city. Its original name was far more poetic: Back in the days when it was prized, it was called the "tree of heaven."

The ghetto palm reminded me of the mourner's biological

impulse to survive. New bereavement research has found that many mourners are highly resilient. Of everyone who suffers a loss, almost ninety percent experience what psychiatrists call normal grief. Most of these people do return to functioning well soon after a loss. But what does being "resilient" mean? The tree of heaven survives its transplantation in the new world; it does so because its roots are deep and grow so quickly. The resilient are the ones who have the most "secure attachments," in psychiatric parlance. Even so, we feel like ghetto palms; the shine of the tree of heaven has rubbed from our leaves.

The way C.'s accent turned "abandoned" into "abundant" got me thinking about whether abandonment can be an opportunity as well as a loss. One part of grief felt like utter abandonment—a sensation of having no place in the world. But I had begun to ask myself whether we were meant to feel that within personal abandonment (if not within the horrific economic abandonment of Detroit) lay a strange abundance: the paradoxical wealth that comes with emptiness. I suppose that Buddhists would understand this, would say, "Of course." With so many beliefs shaken, I could see things freshly; I supposed that somewhere lurking in my loss was the opportunity to create, not unlike the way artists in Detroit were reinhabiting dead buildings and laboriously reconceiving them.

Of course, I was skeptical of this train of thought. It struck me as a form of American "positive thinking" at its most embedded. Yet according to the researcher George

Bonanno, the bereaved often take comfort in what is termed "benefit finding"—a tendency to focus on the so-called silver lining inside the dark cloud. Bonanno notes that people whose loved ones die painfully from cancer often say later, "I am just thankful I had the chance at least to say goodbye."

In the midst of pain, optimism may indeed be a necessary survival tactic. But I wanted to think that the lift I had felt of late was spiritual, not merely predictably psychological.

EIGHT MONTHS after my mother's death, I went back to Marfa to spend some time in the desert before I started teaching again that fall.

On the day of Ted Kennedy's memorial service, Liam called me; he was upset. "These commentators are so dumb," he said. "Can you write something about this? How dumb people are? How little they understand about grief?"

I had no TV in Marfa. "What's up?"

"They are just speculating, they're not thinking. They think they know something, but they're just blithering idiots who work for ABC and who feel free to share their uninformed speculations with the whole nation."

I asked what he meant.

"The way they talk about Kennedy's cancer—it's both sensationalizing and minimizing. They say things like, 'The family has had a year to prepare for this day, and they seem quite calm.' I went on Facebook to post a complaint about how awful this coverage is. I told the guy: You are a dumb commentator who's not thinking about what comes out of your mouth. Prepared? They lost their *father*. Or their *husband*. They are not prepared. He is *dead*. This is a solemn moment, and only they know what they're feeling, not this idiot TV commentator. Everyone's just so freaked out by grief! What do they know? Stop telling us how we feel! Stop speculating!"

Three-quarters of a year after a loss, the hardest part is the permanently transitional quality: you are neither accustomed to it nor in its fresh pangs. You feel you will always be wading the river, your legs burning with exhaustion. Today I wrote a note to someone who just lost her father. In it, without thought, I began to write, *The loss doesn't pass, but the anguish does—it subsides*. Then I thought: Who am I to say?

I returned to New York last week, where memories suffused every corner. Having dinner with Jodie, I said something about how I need to move forward, not look back.

"But you are moving forward."

"What do you mean?"

"You're meeting people who didn't know your mother and developing relationships with them. You might wish they knew your mother, but you get to know them, you do it in good faith. You're moving forward."

But it had started to feel untenable, the memories everywhere. The next day, on a run, we were going past the school where my mother worked, when I saw two administrators walking up the block toward us. They stopped to ask me how I was, to see how my father was, to say we should get together. I answered, explained, agreed. As we turned from them to get coffee, we ran into Diana, who's now head of admissions at Saint Ann's. Jodie knew her from my wedding and from the memorial service. We waved. As we crossed the street Jodie said: "Point taken. Maybe you should move to Manhattan."

I HAD TRIED to find a metaphor for my loss in the weeks after my mother's death. Lately I have been thinking about a different metaphor: a metaphor for the self after loss. We have a word for the wife who's lost her husband—widow—but it's not a metaphor; it's an identity. And we don't really have a word for having lost a parent—except when we speak of children who have lost both parents as "orphaned." Walking to a party in Tribeca the other night—on one of those smoky, resonant autumn evenings—I caught a glimpse of my face in the window of a hotel. I was thinking about how hard it was to say how much I missed my mother, yet how central the feeling was. It is heartsickness, like the sadness you feel after a breakup, but many times stronger and more desperate. I miss her: I want to talk to her, hear her voice, have a joke with her. I am willing for us to be "broken up" if she'll just have dinner with me once. And as I was walking I thought: *I will carry this wound forever.* It's not a question of getting over it or healing. No; it's a question of learning to live with this transformation. For the loss is transformative, in good ways and bad, a tangle of change that cannot be threaded into the usual narrative spools. It is too central for that. It's not an emergence from the cocoon, but a tree growing around an obstruction.

CHAPTER THIRTEEN

the return of the dead

Suddenly it was fall, the season of death, the anniversary of things-going-to-hell. Because Halloween fell on a Saturday, the day had an especially festive quality, with more people out on the streets in the daylight. I passed a caveman couple with their Superman son. A sexy kitty mom accompanied a young vampire of five or so.

I was struck by how few ghosts and goblins there were. In Mexico, November 2 is celebrated as the Day of the Dead. The holiday is an occasion to remember and venerate the dead, to give them their proper due. People build altars honoring the deceased. They visit graves with marigolds and sugar skulls and the deceased's favorite foods, much the way the Egyptians did in the Beautiful Feast of the Valley. By contrast, the American Halloween is mostly about candy and horror films. Even the plastic ghosts fluttering from door-ways seem goofy rather than ghoulish.

One Halloween, when I was about seven, my mother was irritable after school and took a short nap before we went trick-or-treating. I got that crestfallen feeling children get. I was going to be a bad fairy, but I had no wand. Looking around, I spied my father's Szechuan peppers drying on the door, upside down. I broke one off, bright red, slick with the oil of its spices, and wrapped it in a funnel of tinfoil. Sometimes in those days my father would try to amuse me by wrapping tinfoil into a ball and telling me it contained magic.

No, I'd say.

Yes, he'd insist.

There's no magic in there. How did you get magic in there?

That is what tinfoil is for. We wrap leftovers in it, but it's really for capturing magic. Be careful, though: you can't open it, because the magic will be gone. And you might need it later. Magic is hard to catch, so we should save this one.

No . . . I said.

But I was convinced. I kept that ball of tinfoil carefully against my side all night.

So tonight, remembering the magic tinfoil, I decided the base of my wand would be tinfoil. The hot pepper on top.

My mother woke up.

Let me show you my wand, I said.

OK, she said drowsily.

It's really cool. Look.

She looked and started laughing. That's clever, Meg. Very original.

And that was my magic.

It was a warm fall and there were more leaves on the trees than usual. As a friend and I walked home from a birthday party she nudged me and said, "Oh, look! They're already putting up the winter holiday decorations." I looked up, and there was a large electric snowflake strung across the street. "It's a little early, no?" she continued, unaware of the effect it was having on me. "Yes," I said. "It's a little early."

A FEW WEEKS EARLIER, on a late-summer day when even the grass had been burning in the sun, I'd received a condolence note—an e-mail—from a man who'd known my mother in grade school. I had never heard of this man. His shock that she was dead emanated from the note. My curiosity piqued, I wrote back to ask if he had any stories to share of my mother as a girl. Just the week before, I'd read that the newly bereaved often crave more information about the dead—stories that show sides of the person you didn't know. Anytime I heard a new story about my mother, it was like she was alive again. She was still capable of generating novelty! So perhaps she was not quite dead.

It is said, too, that daughters are particularly keen to learn more about their dead mothers. Whatever the case, D. had stories but wanted to share them in person. We met a few months after e-mailing, on a rainy Friday morning, by a building that had been destroyed on 9/11 and then rebuilt. The week before, he'd called our meeting off because he had to think it over, but today he showed up—a tall man with sandy gray hair; you could see the boy still in his loping walk. He worked at Ground Zero, overseeing some reconstruction, and he'd planned a tour to break the ice, then coffee.

As we walked around he described the progress of foundation laying in the east and west "bathtubs," or the footprints of the old buildings. The scope of the work was extraordinary. Pointing out the crane at work on one of the towers, he noted, "That's the biggest crane anyone has ever used. And see those baskets hanging off the girders? That's a new technique, one developed just to work with these girders. They're designed to withstand the kind of fireball that took down the Twin Towers. Buildings this secure have never been made."

We stood, taking in the scene.

"You look like your father's side of the family," D. observed suddenly. "You don't have that Kelly black hair." We were passing Dey Street, and he paused and waved to a heavyset man bent over a drill in the midst of a construction crew.

"Hey, Tommy," D. called out to him. "Tommy!" The man came over, breaking into a smile. They hugged and kissed.

D. says, "Let me introduce you. This is Meghan O'Rourke. She's Barbara O'Rourke's—Barbara Kelly's—daughter."

"Barbara Kelly," Tommy repeats, lighting up. "No kiddin'!" I recognize his accent. "How's Barbara? How's your mother doin'?"

I started to change my facial expression—something I realized I always do—when D. put his hand on my shoulder and said, gently, "She passed away, Tommy. She passed away last year."

Tommy's face changed. "Ah, I'm so sorry. Your mother, she was a great lady, she was a blast," he said, squeezing my hand. "She also did well in school. I didn't, as you can tell!"

At a deli down the block, the owner knew D. well. "Sit down, sit down," he said, as we walked in, and he brought coffee and urged food on D., who waved it off. "I can't eat. I have a story I have to tell."

As I ate a sandwich, D. started to talk slowly.

It had been forty years since he last saw my mother. They had gone to Catholic school together in New Jersey, back when their town was different: more Catholic, more insular, more old-fashioned. He was unpopular, she was popular; he was a bad student, she was a good student; he was a football player, she was a cheerleader. She was part of a clique he didn't much like. Once, before he got to know her, he'd gone to Holmdel Park, where all the boys and girls paired up in an elaborate, orchestrated ritual organized by the girls, and walked along various paths, and my mother had somehow ended up with him. Then, at a dance, she approached him while "Hey Jude" was playing and asked him to dance. Later it played again, and my mother went up to him a second time, and, as he put it, "in her direct, Barbara way, she said, 'So you're going to dance with me again, right?'"

I interrupted to ask what the other girls were like, and he said, slowly, "There was no one like your mother."

They grew close. They told each other everything, walking home from school carrying books, talking on the phone for hours. On the school trip to the Museum of Natural History in New York, my mother lingered with D. and explained all the exhibits to him. She was sharp, he said, but you wouldn't know it unless you were friends with her; she was not a show-off in class. At another dance they walked out from the party and held hands in the courtyard. He felt it was like she had sensed that he wanted to be alone with her—not to do anything, but just to be away from the pack.

In class, he struggled with reading, so my mother arranged to sit next to him—she could make things happen, as he put it. When it was his turn to read, she would read the words under her breath to guide him. "She always leaned way too close," he said. "I was sure the nuns would notice." He wasn't always a good student, and one day he heard a nun say, "Barbara Kelly should not be hanging out with the likes of that boy."

Her friends also didn't like that they were spending so much time together. One summer day they were at the beach club when a popular boy picked a fight with D., who was sitting next to my mother; the boy told D. to move away and make room. The fight put D. in a terrible mood; he felt this marked the beginning of the end of their friendship. But my mother asked him to take a swim with her. She swam out much farther than he was comfortable with, but she was very athletic. They stayed in the ocean for an hour, talking, sitting on the rope buoys, her dark hair blowing across her face. Her lips got blue. He told her they should go in, but she said, Let's just sit out here a while longer. They sat together under the big sky, listening to the cries of the birds.

As time went on, as he told it, older boys were becoming annoyed that my mother paid D. so much attention. In football practice, one tackled him purposefully hard and broke his wrist. D. was benched. He had to go to the games and watch my mother cheer for all the other players. That was hard; it had always felt like something between them that she was a cheerleader and he was on the team. But during the game, she looked up at him as he sat on the bleachers.

At some point soon after, he began to drift away, having decided there was no way to stay friends. Without football, he was having a bad time, and he started getting kicked out of class for talking back to the nuns. One day my mother stopped at his locker and said, "I don't like what I'm hearing about what's going on with you. Are you OK?" And he said, "Yes," and walked away. She tried again later. "Why don't we talk anymore?" she asked, stopping at his locker again; he didn't respond. She looked extremely hurt, he told me, but he closed his locker and walked away, thinking he would never forget the look on her face. And he hadn't.

Soon after, my mother left to go to the public school in town. He saw her only one more time. She had already met my father and was at Barnard; home for a visit, she was picking her sisters up from a dance. He was hanging out in the parking lot with some friend. One said, "Barbara Kelly is inside, you should say hi." And he said, "No, I can't." Then he thought, What the hell, why not? We can have the last conversation we should have had. I can explain what really happened. He found her and he said hello. And she just looked at him. Then she turned around and left. That was the last time he saw her.

It was funny: He had always wanted to get out of the town as soon as he could. But it was my mom who left, while he stayed, living two blocks from their school. He told me he never speaks of this period of his life, but last year his father had died and a bunch of old friends wrote to him, asking him to get together with them. He stopped to think about why he always pushed these friends away, and, he told me, "Barbara flashed into my mind, and I thought that if I could just make that girl laugh once more, everything would be OK."

He knew from another friend that she worked at Saint Ann's. He googled her to get her number, to tell her he wanted to give her a tour of Ground Zero. Instead, up came the *New York Times* notice: *The entire Saint Ann's family mourns the loss of Barbara O'Rourke, friend, colleague and teacher, and extends its profound sympathies to Paul, Meghan, Liam and Eamon.*

Memories flooded him, memories he couldn't push away. Every night when he walked the dog—just blocks away from their old haunts—he thought of my mother. So one day he wrote to me, half thinking I would write back to tell him it was all a huge misunderstanding. After all, there was no way the girl he had known, and always meant to apologize to, was simply gone. It had seemed there would be time for one last meeting, one last conversation, one last chance to talk about the bond that had once been between them.

He had a photo he wanted to give me. It showed a bare-foot girl with long legs sitting next to a gangly thirteen-year-old boy whose arm is in a cast. "She came to visit me when I was injured," he told me, "and wouldn't let anyone else sit next to me." Her hair is black and neat. Her features look etched, as if she is more painted than real.

He said, "I don't know why, but I have been haunted by your mother's death ever since I found out about it. I didn't feel this upset when my father died." As we left the deli, we paused once more to look down at the footprint of the towers. And he told me one more thing. His sons played soccer in Holmdel Park, where he and my mother walked that first day. In the park, the trees are mostly hardwood. But there is one part where there is a stand of pines, and the path becomes soft. One day during their practice he went back around the paths and there they were, the pines, and Barbara came vividly to his mind. He doesn't know why. Maybe she said something about them. Whatever it was, it's gone. But whenever he sees the pines alone there among the hardwoods, he thinks of the girl he once knew, and their long-ago friendship.

As I walked home over the Brooklyn Bridge, I was wrapped in a languorous, uneasy exhaustion. That vision of her in the pines, I reflected, was the true ghost, the haunting that Halloween's false ghosts only parody. Home, I got in bed and slept for three hours, as if I'd been on a taxing trip and needed rest.

O NE OF THE GRUBBY TRUTHS about a loss is that you don't just mourn the dead person, you mourn the person you got to be when the lost one was alive. This loss might even be what affects you most. Jim kept saying, "I am sorry for all the things your mother is going to miss"—and he would list them. And I would think: I am a sorry excuse for a daughter. I just think about how I miss her. I'm sorry for myself, sorry about losing a life where I always had a mom to go to. Whatever the case, in grief you're not just reconstituting the lost person, recalling her, then letting her go—you're having to grow into the shocking new role you play on a planet without her. One night Liam said to me, as we were driving home from my dad's to Brooklyn, "I am not as sad as I was, but the thing is, it's just less fun and less good without her." I only now have begun to understand what that means. The main difference is that I'm the only woman in a family of men—a father and two brothers. That this shift came with a certain caretaking aspect, whether I willed it or not, was underscored at my mother's funeral. My father spoke about how my mother had cut his hair since he was twenty-three, when they got married. Afterward, her sister Joanne came up to me and said, "Now *you're* going to have to cut his hair!"

No way. Off he went to the barber the next week.

But that first fall, I found myself making a point of having lunch, talking with him about selling the house. He talked about buying a smaller house, deeper in the countryside. He was sixty-three. I had disastrous visions of his getting sick three years from now and going through the whole goddamn thing again, only now he would be an hour from any hospital and two hours from the city. So I said, Wouldn't you maybe prefer to rent a place closer to the train station, closer to the city, so we can all visit easily? By the end of lunch he'd come around to this idea. I could see that my mother was dead. In the past he'd never have listened to me like that. In a tiny way I was becoming my mother—and that was not just a melancholic identification. We take on parts of the role the person played.

Part of my new role is to worry. I have a twenty-one-year-old brother who no longer has a mother and who hasn't graduated from college. He started teaching part-time at Pierrepont and living with my dad. He wants eventually to transfer to a new college, but sometimes this plan seems vaguely distant. And I find that I think about him, worry about him. I call my father to say, "We need to figure out his college applications." I come by the house and say, "Kiddo, don't you need to wash your hair?" And, "I think he needs a desk and a dresser in his room." And, "Don't you want a plate to eat that off?" My father does everything he is capable of, but he's in his own grief.

"I just feel like I'm standing in place, and everyone else, all my friends, they're moving on," Eamon said to me one day, the fall after her death. I told him, "No, not at all—you're young. Your whole life is in front of you. You just need to figure out what you want to do—apply to school, travel, what." He was sitting next to me at the school my mother used to help run, watercoloring a poster he made for the door of his classroom. He had drawn a castle and moat, a deep moat, with a dragon attacking it from on high. Around the castle he'd printed all the names of the kids in the class.

"Yeah," he said. The paintbrush scratched over the print. "I don't know."

But I was telling him partial lies. Because his friends *are* moving on, many of them with their mothers and fathers at their backs, giving them allowances, helping them buy clothes, showing up at graduation with gifts and flowers, and when he should have been preparing to leave school he was in a hospital saying, I think they're giving her too much Ativan, too much morphine.

What are the last words of hers that Eamon remembers? After she died he went red-eyed into the living room and curled up on the couch and wrote in his notebook. Later he left it open and I saw in his handwriting, still so like a little boy's, large-lettered and round, MOM DIED TODAY. SHE . . . and I stopped reading, I picked up the notebook and closed it and put it to the side before the funeral. That night after her death—after that Christmas dinner I barely remember—I found him on the couch looking at a picture of her and him when he was three, the two of them on boogie boards on Cape Cod, and they're tan and he's all blond hair and baby curls and blue eyes and he's grinning as children do and she is smiling as mothers do and the ocean sweeps around them, foaming and aquamarine, and you can almost see it move. He was hitting his hand to his forehead over and over. I went over and I took the picture from his hands and I said, I know you need to feel this, but I think you need to go to sleep right now, darling. It's late and you're exhausted. The picture will be here tomorrow. And he let me slip the picture from his hands and give him water and an Ativan.

Now he was silent and curved away from me over the drawing.

I didn't know you could draw so well, I said, lamely.

Yeah, he said.

A few months after my mother died I was reading a memoir by my great-uncle David, my grandfather's youngest brother, a priest who lives in Berkeley. In it he wrote that he was "especially aware of having moved from the ground rules of one world into a new world with completely different rules." These new rules were connected to "a sense of entitlement":

Young people today believe that they are entitled. Entitled to the good life, entitled to live without frustration, entitled to a sense of personal fulfillment, entitled to sexual relationships without personal entanglements. . . . I live and work in this world. But I feel like a tourist. In effect, I have become an outsider.

I realized it was what I'd been feeling—*I have suddenly become an outsider among my peers.* Because many had not gone through a terrible loss or a major illness, they were still operating as planners, coordinators, under the star of entitlement, from which I had been abruptly banished. I had felt that, however benignly or unconsciously, the world around me wanted my grief stifled and silenced; it threatened a particular lie of the moment and class I lived in, the myth of self-improvement and control, the myth of meritocratic accomplishment leading to happiness and security. I drew close to those who'd gone through an experience that ruptured this way of seeing the world, because those who hadn't often left me feeling keenly alone. A year after my mother died, my friend Jodie's father was in the hospital; I told a mutual friend, who went silent, then said, "You always think these things are going to happen to someone else, but I guess that one day they're going to happen to us." I didn't know how to respond.

My first memory is of waking up from a dream about balloons, a street fair, being on my father's shoulders. My mother comes into the room. *Where was the parade we went to last night?* I ask her. *Hmm?* she says, pulling my pajamas over my head. *We went to a parade.* The cotton shirt lassoes my arms. No, honey, that was a dream, she says.

Some days still, the memories come. And I can't read, or think, or do anything but want her.

In my mind, Thanksgiving marked the beginning of the end of my mother's life. I had a cold hollow in my stomach thinking about its arrival. A few days before, I went for a walk on the Brooklyn Bridge, looking out over the metallic water. Gazing out beyond the Statue of Liberty and the Buttermilk Channel to the Verrazano, beyond the loading docks and derricks, I felt, viscerally, the interweaving of industry and nature and people, the layers of history. It helped me slip out of the grip of obdurate individuality and into the grip of something larger: a sense that I was part of a system. That morning I had reread a section of John Ashbery's "The New Spirit":

> Because life is short
> We must remember to keep asking it the same question
> Until the repeated question and the same silence become
>   answer
> In words broken open and pressed to the mouth
> And the last silence reveal the lining

Until at last this thing exist separately
At all levels of the landscape and in the sky . . .

Walking home, thinking about the silent changes that had occurred in me over the last year, I reached the intersection of Atlantic Avenue and Court. As I stood at the light I heard a thud. Something feathery rolled along the hood of a black sedan to my right and hit the ground, and there were feathers, a leg, another leg—had the driver hit a pigeon?—and even as I wondered, the feathers slowed into a tawny hugeness and the thing rolled over and I saw amber eyes look at me and blink. It was a hawk—a large, magnificent hawk. Struggling to raise itself up, it shook its wings but fell back. It lay panting on the pavement two feet from me, huge, badly hurt. I began to shake. Seeing it jostled some sensation loose in me that had been tamped down since my mother's death—the panic of witnessing vulnerability, a creature struggling not to die.

The car that hit it drove on. Now the light was red. A man advanced into the traffic and waved at the bird. I stepped into the street and waved, too, as if it could be shooed. It strained but couldn't get off the ground. "Come on," I said, powerless. Cars were honking and people were turning to stare and the traffic pressed forward. What should I do? What could I do? Could I call 911? Confusedly, I stepped back on the sidewalk and called Jim. "There's a hawk in the street," I said nonsensically, crying, as if he could do something about it. The man nudged it again and then the light changed once more and the cars surged forward. "Oh no," I said. "Oh no."

But as I held the phone to my ear the hawk strained once again and this time it lifted up, unfurling its long wings and rising, heading from the ground to the sky majestically. "What's happening?" Jim said. "It's flying," I said. Hanging low, it looped to the left and changed direction. "It's flying. I don't know if it's OK, but it's flying." And I hung up and ran after to see, still shaking. One minute it had been on the ground, wounded, mortal, and the next it had risen, and a burden lifted from my shoulders.

Thanksgiving itself was cloudy and mild. I bought apples for pie at the local store before driving up with my brothers; the Brooklyn streets were quiet, as after a storm. Worried about my father being alone, we arrived at his house in the late morning. He was glad to see us. The rest of our guests—Emily, our cousin Rachel, her husband, Doug, and their two-year-old daughter, Sasha—arrived in the mid-afternoon. We began cooking, and I found that in the chopping of apples and the smells there was a strange, pleasurable tug of connection to the past.

Earlier that year, I had had to make an apple pie for a video for the Web magazine about the everyday lessons mothers teach their daughters. The idea filled me with dread, and for a day or two before I made the pie I was gloomy, resentful that I had to make this pie, a pie I wished she were teaching me to make once again.

On the day of the shoot, I pulled out the old recipe book my mother and father had given my brothers and me—the

4A Cookbook, they called it, after the apartment we lived in. And, step-by-step, I made the pie. I didn't let the dough chill for long enough and it came apart as I tried to roll it out. The result looked messier than usual. But it had been strangely comforting to read my mother's words and revisit her way of making things. At the end of the recipe for pastry (butter, Crisco, flour, sugar, water) she had written, philosophically: "This will constitute the dough," a phrasing I would never have paid much attention to in the past. As the pie was cooking, I got flustered. I was supposed to turn the heat down from 425 degrees. But to what temperature? I reached for the phone. And realized—I couldn't. From now on, I would have to answer my pie questions myself, through trial and error.

Afterward, I called my dad and asked him why he thought making the pie had brought me so close to my mother. He listened, then said, "A few months ago, you were talking about how you were envious of cultures where there are rituals for mourning. And it just seems to me that within our family, when things happened, whether good or bad, we tended to get together. And when we got together, we ate together, which meant cooking. So you learned from your mother how to make pie. It is a concrete thing she gave you. But it's also that when you make it, you are part of a tradition. Someday you're going to be the person to teach someone else."

I told him about the impulse to call her, and he said something that stayed with me. "The making of the pie *is* the phone call. To make pie was to call your mom." Then he added, "Come Thanksgiving, you've got to make the apple pie."

"What do you mean *I've got to*?" I asked.

"Well, the common thing across societies is this idea of yearly commemoration—Easter, the empty chair at the Seder, the Egyptian festival called the Beautiful Feast of the Valley, when the Thebans crossed the Nile to picnic at the mortuaries that held their ancestors and recent dead. It's almost like forced remembrance. So next Thanksgiving, you've got to make the apple pie."

And so here I was on Thanksgiving, making the pie. With family around, cooking the same things we always cooked, creating the same smells we'd always created, my mother's death no longer seemed a bleak marker of "Before" and "After." I felt her absence around us but I also saw how, too, she was embedded in us.

The next day, a couple and their daughter came to see the house, which now, to my shock, had a For Sale sign outside. They walked around and asked questions; upon entering, the realtor asked me, "Are you the owner?" "No, I'm their—his daughter," I said, stumblingly. "The owner is Paul, my father." As the realtor talked to my father, the family wandered through, opening cupboards, peering into my mother's study. "This is cute!" the wife said. "It's like a little study, it could be my work room." They wandered back into the dining room.

"We'd want to put a pool back there," the husband said, gesturing to the part of the yard where my parents had planned on putting one. "So why is your dad leaving?"

"I think he has too much space," I said, semi-truthfully.

III

anniversaries

I knew that a Christmas carol would make me cry this season. I just didn't know it would be "Frosty the Snowman," that least dignified of all carols, the Asti Spumante to the Champagne of "Silent Night." I was driving to Trader Joe's on a rainy Sunday to buy poinsettias and eggnog for a small party I was having. As I distractedly pressed the radio buttons, I heard the familiar bumptious chorus, and my stomach turned with nostalgia: "Thumpety thump thump, thumpety thump thump, look at Frosty go." But it was when Frosty, knowing of his imminent demise, tells the kids, "Let's run, and we'll have some fun now, before I melt away," that tears leaked down my face.

The holidays brought a feeling of togetherness that my mother loved. After Christmas, before going back to school, she would sit for days on the couch reading the books she'd been given, playing with a new camera, and take us for walks with the dogs, imbued with joy at the week's quiet wintriness. Though my parents never had much money, she always went overboard, searching out gifts that we didn't know we wanted.

I still can't bear the idea of anyone knowing she is about to die, least of all my mother. Last year at this time, she was climbing the stairs with me to the attic to gather the Christmas decorations. She had already had radiation surgery for her brain tumors, but it had left her weak and confused (and on the verge of descending into a steroidal delirium) and she kept trying to pick up full, heavy boxes and carry them downstairs.

"Mom, put the box down."

"But I want to decorate."

"I know, but we don't need all that."

"But I want *all* the decorations," she said, stubbornly.

It was like managing a child. As I turned away, she picked up a large box containing the heavy tree stand, and, when she caught me looking at her, regarded me with truculent defiance. I realized that my idea of decorating the house while my brothers and father were at school was a bad one. Wanting to get my mother away from the television, I'd built up a Norman Rockwell vision of cozy togetherness, in which hanging up the old red ribbons and the white lights could stave off the death that was sniffing around our house, looking for a point of entrance. But she was far too confused and fragile for this exercise in nostalgia.

She was living gamely despite her approaching death and it hobbled my heart. I still find it terrifying to imagine. It is like picturing one's slow self-erasure, noticing the disappearance, one day, of a pinkie, the next of a toe, then slowly, all the toes, all the fingers, a hand.

I have been thinking of a story my mother used to tell me when I was a little girl. I loved baths and resisted getting out. One day, when I was about three, my mother, impatient, said, "If you stay in the bath any longer, you'll turn into a raisin."

"No I won't."

"Look at your fingertips."

I looked. They were wrinkled and pruny.

"That's just my fingers. Fingers always wrinkle."

"You don't know the story of the little girl who turned into a raisin?" my mother asked, holding up a towel.

"No."

"There was a little girl in New York who loved to take baths. She never wanted to get out when her mother asked her to. One day, her mother asked her over and over to get out, but the little girl wouldn't. So her mother threw up her hands and went downstairs. The little girl kept playing, but she was getting smaller and smaller. First her fingers and toes wrinkled up, then her hands and feet, then her whole body, until she had shrunk to a raisin. Her mother came upstairs and looked for her but she wasn't in the bath. 'Oh, she must have gotten out,' the mother said, and she pulled the plug out of the drain. 'Oh no!' cried the girl, but her mother couldn't hear her. And as the bath water swirled out of the bath, so, too, did the little girl, going down the drain."

"Was she OK?"

"She went down the drain and out the house through the pipes under the streets and came up in a grate on the street. Meanwhile, her mother and father searched for her everywhere, very upset. They wanted their little girl back! But they couldn't find her. The next evening they went to a friend's house and passed the grate where the girl was lying. It was a very quiet night and as the mother walked she thought she heard something. She looked down. 'Look, it's a raisin,' she said to her husband. 'How strange!' and she picked it up. It moved in her hands and when she looked she saw it was their little girl. She cried with joy and went inside and took out a hair dryer and dried the raisin girl until slowly she plumped back up, first her fingers and toes, then her hands and feet, until she was herself again."

My mother gave me her look. "Now do you want to get out?"

"Yes!" I said.

And I stepped out into the scratchy old white towel and her arms came around my body.

I KNOW I need to do something with your mother's clothes," my father said to me one night after dinner. "I just don't know what to do. I started to look through them and I thought OK, all this can go. But then I found some formal clothes, and I thought, I can't just go dump these at

Goodwill. I have memories of your mother wearing them, at Saint Ann's events, at parties, at weddings"—mercifully he didn't say "at *your* wedding"—"and it seems odd to just leave them there with everything else."

"Do you want to keep them?" I said.

"Yes, I want to keep some, just to, just to," he faltered, "have." He rubbed his hair, which is fine and soft, like a duckling's, a pale white that could almost be a newborn's blond corona. "I also want to do this *mindfully*, and I don't think that just dropping all of her stuff off at Goodwill is mindful. It seems mindless," he said. "I want people to have things of hers. I just don't know how to do it. I don't want to do anything rash."

Holding on indefinitely to the possessions of the dead, and keeping rooms just as the dead left them, are symptoms of complicated or pathological grief, I'd learned. That my father was thinking about letting go of her clothes was a good sign. He hadn't cleaned out her closet or her study, though he didn't seem finicky about keeping her possessions exactly in place. Mostly, he just seemed overwhelmed. "We could help you," I said. "We could take stuff to Goodwill for you."

"Oh, I have no problem taking stuff to Goodwill," he replied. "I don't find it upsetting or anything. I just don't know what to do."

I thought how different men and women are—how clear it was that he did find it upsetting, but simply wouldn't say so. Even knowing this, I was hurt to hear him say that dumping my mother's possessions at the Goodwill didn't upset him. *It is upsetting,* I thought. *And you should be able to say so.* We're always judging one another, we mourners.

M Y M O T H E R had given me a novel for Christmas many years ago, which I found myself wanting to reread, about a young woman who loses her father, whom she's been taking care of for eleven years. Because she is devastated by the prospect of losing love again, she prefers to retreat than risk love. It is easier to live in emotional hiding than with the likelihood of a future heartbreak.

I remembered the book on one of those days when I thought how easy it would be to lie around sleeping and eating mindlessly for the rest of my life. I wanted to reread the end of the novel, where the heroine who has grown depressed in her seclusion decides to reject her fearful penitence and return to a life of pleasure—to sex, to love, to her friends, to the chance of joy. But I couldn't find the copy my mother had given me. One night, walking home from teaching, I saw an old paperback copy of it on a dollar table on Sixth Avenue and bought it. I read it that night, feeling I was understanding both something about my experience and my mother's, since she had loved that book. I think I will always look for clues to her in books and photographs. A mourner is always searching for traces of the lost one because they bear testimonial force: This person existed.

We were now in the anniversary of the last week of her life. On my way uptown to meet my friend Anat, my childhood best friend, who was in town from Palo Alto to see a play, I did some shopping, meandering down to the West Village to Three Lives, the kind of bookstore we used to all browse in for hours as a family, where my mother would slowly introduce us to the books she had loved and now thought we should read. Looking at a book about science and the Enlightenment, I thought how much it would interest her. "It's perfect," I decided. "I'll get it." Then I remembered. But still I thought, stupidly: *Surely if I buy it for her, she will read it.*

"Anniversary reactions" are common among mourners on any date that reminds them of the loved one: birthdays, holidays, and especially the first anniversary of a death. One study found that people are often admitted to the hospital on the anniversary of a death, even many years later. But in the days leading up to Christmas, I had been sleeping better than I had all year. I went to friends' holiday parties in a daze of gratitude that I was not "numbed out." I found myself picking up the old routines, putting on makeup, realizing I had to go to the gym. I felt lightness again, a true sense of savoring the everyday, especially when I saw Anat, whom I'd known since I was twelve. My mother had been instrumental in our friendship. As the principal of the middle school, she'd assigned me to be Anat's "guide" on the first day of seventh grade, when she was a new student. I apparently started talking, quite fast, as soon as we met, and didn't stop all day. We have been close since then. Peculiarly, it happened that the play we went to had been written by an old colleague of my mother's and was about the anniversary of a death. It seemed as if the universe were conspiring to show me: Look! People move on. Or perhaps these signs had been there all along, only now my brain was ready to see them.

After we had dinner, I walked home from the subway in a snowstorm, past all the houses with their holiday decorations. I snapped a photo on my phone of the snow falling through the holiday lights by the brownstones. The snow was falling so fast that in the picture the flakes resembled scores of ghostly tiny comets streaking to the mantled ground. What if our minds are cameras set to a narrow aperture, unable to perceive the full reality around us, and we are in the midst of a complicated storm, one that is ongoing, dynamic, imperceptible? And what if my mother were in that storm? It was in the haze of such chimeras that I found hope.

I also found myself seeing freshly all the ways our family had changed. A few days before Christmas, Isabel mentioned that Eamon had had an epileptic seizure. No one in my family had told me, and I was annoyed. As my father and I talked on the phone, my annoyance erupted and I snapped at him. He snapped back, his voice rising. I knew I was doing exactly what I shouldn't do—I knew I was being hard on my father—but he was the center of the family now. I needed him to tell us what was happening, the way my mother would have told us. Of course, this line of thinking was fruitless: he would never be my mother.

In the past, we might have hung up still angry. (A year earlier, while my mother was sick, my father had done exactly that, cutting me off mid-sentence; infuriated, I told my mother I would never speak to him again.) Today, we both paused, and backed down.

"I don't want to fight with you," I finally said.

"I should have called," he said, quietly. "It's just hard to remember all the things your mother used to do."

On Christmas Eve, our father came to the door looking tired and happy to see us. He had been searching the cupboards for canned tomatoes to make the traditional Christmas Eve pizza. Our Christmases had always been heavily ritualized in a secular manner. Every year, we went to a movie and then my father made pizza as we wrapped gifts. This year we hadn't made it to the movie—we got home too late—but we were going to have the pizza. Except my father had forgotten to buy tomatoes. I went upstairs to wrap presents, and Liam came in my room twenty minutes later to tell me that our father, who had gone to get more tomatoes, had just called to say none of the stores were open. I said maybe we could order pizza.

"I doubt anywhere is open. That's the difference between Fairfield and Brooklyn. Poor dad. He must be upset."

We went downstairs to see what else we could eat, but found only some cheese and crackers, stale cereal, canned soup, and puckering red peppers. It was getting late when our father finally returned. He'd found tomatoes after driving around for an hour. The next day, he told Liam, "Last night, when I couldn't find the tomatoes for the pizza, I just thought, 'I ruined everything. I was trying to make Christmas go on, but I failed.'"

As the sauce simmered, we belatedly gathered to decorate the tree, which felt comforting and terrifying at once. My father always had preferred to listen to Renaissance carols—it went with his affection for old cultures—but my mother had loved carols sung by Sinatra or Bing Crosby, so he cleaned a scratch on a *Christmas with the Rat Pack* CD and put it on. Everything had become fodder for nostalgia.

My parents had collected Christmas ornaments for years, and as we rummaged through the boxes we came across ornament after ornament our mother had handpicked. They were like bridges to the past: the plastic replicas of Secretariat and Smarty Jones she'd purchased from the New York Racing Association; a mummy for our father; numerous deer and the feathered birds she favored, some looking the worse for wear. And then there were the misshapen felt ornaments we had made with our mother's help—we would go to the Woolworth's on Court Street and pick out felt, glitter pens, and sequins. Holiday joy now comes with shards of pain.

Soon the pizza—oily, with sharp cheddar cheese on top—was ready. Eamon called out, "Dad, where are you?" as my father fussed in the kitchen. We sat together for dinner, one fewer plate at the table. I had spent so much of this week avoiding thinking about my mother, and I was doing it even as we sat there. The mind is like an ocean that we sometimes look into, and sometimes not, staring at the sun, distracted by the clamorous beach around us. I noticed that my father had a bad cough. Huck, our golden retriever, anxiously licked our feet under the table, as if sensing the odd energy in the air.

But something about being together was buoying. After dinner, I persuaded my brothers to watch *Scrooged* instead of a goofy boy comedy; we'd watched it back in 2005, the Christmas before my mother received the diagnosis, when we still could find safety in the bright shadow of holiday promise. Now we piled on the couch where my mom used to rest after her chemo. Huck squeezed in among us and licked our feet, and our father sat on the edge of the fireplace. After a bit he went up to bed. We watched together, a makeshift family: the siblings and the dog.

Christmas was cloudy. I woke early and went downstairs to make tea. As I passed my father's open bedroom door, I saw a large, square white cardboard container on a side table. My heart beating faster, I went in. The box bore a plain label that read, in neat type, BARBARA JEAN KELLY O'ROURKE. If the box had always been there, I had managed never to see it. Now, the morning of the anniversary of her death, I recognized it as the container of my mother's ashes.

My father was sitting in the living room—the room where my mother died—wrapping presents. It had the air of a stage set. I was sniffling from the dog.

"Do you have any more Claritin?"

"I don't know. Is there any in the cabinet?"

I rummaged around, but all that was in the cabinet was stale food and old receipts for my mother's medicine. There was no Claritin. If my mother were alive, there would be Claritin when I came home, and tissues everywhere, and she would have vacuumed the house herself even after the cleaning lady did. My mother was not obsessed with cleanliness. But that was one of the things she did for me. She vacuumed up the dog hair.

"I guess there's none," my father said.

"Well, next time you go to the grocery, could you buy some, so there's some always around the house?" I said.

"I'm sorry," he said, real sorrow in his voice. I felt like a total jerk. Here was my father, himself grieving, taking care of my youngest brother and all of us, trying to sell his house in a bad market, worried about money, approaching the age of retirement—and I was complaining that he hadn't bought Claritin so I could feel parented? It was time to grow up.

"It's OK. I should have brought some. I forgot."

"No, I should have it in the house," he said, looking tired.

By the time I got back from the gas station, travel packs of Claritin in hand, my brothers were up. "We still haven't come downstairs!" Liam said. This was an old ritual that we'd extended preposterously into the present day, mostly because Eamon was so much younger than Liam and I: we stayed upstairs and came down with our eyes closed, so our mother could take pictures of us as we saw the heap of gifts under the tree. Eamon would always anticipate how many gifts there would be.

"How big is the pile going to be, Mom?" he'd say.

"I don't know. Pretty small," she'd say.

"No!" he'd cry out. "There will be mountains!"

Somehow the whole morning was a pleasure—maybe it was just that we were distracted by the joy of stuff. But rather than merely feel my mother's absence, I was buoyed by the fact that we were all there, by the small gestures of kindness and love that glued the morning together. It was as joyous as it could have been.

We'd made plans to drive to New York to scatter my mother's ashes in Prospect Park—where she had loved to walk our dogs—and have lunch at a quiet restaurant. But as my father started to make breakfast, we realized that we didn't really want to go to the restaurant. "That's fine," I said, a surge of anxiety in my stomach at the thought that we might not observe her death. "But I think we should scatter some of her ashes anyway. I feel the need to do something. It seems weird to sit here with our stuff as if nothing happened."

"We'll go to the beach," Dad said.

"Can we go at three, when she died?"

Eamon looked away. He was upset. I could see that part of him didn't want to deal with the ashes, but wanted just to have Christmas—to siphon what joy he could from our being together, from his new gifts, like a mariner decanting drinkable water from the sea. He wanted to relax and let the holiday be a holiday. Looking up, he said to me, "I'd like more time to sit around. Can we at least come back here afterward, before driving down?"

"Of course," I said, pained that he even had to ask.

THEY TOOK my mother's body away so quickly. There we all were, touching her, hugging her, kissing her, saying goodbye. A year ago. For twenty minutes she was warm and she didn't look dead. She didn't look alive either. But she didn't have the glazed, absent expression I had expected. Her being seemed present. I could feel it hovering at the ceiling of the room, changing, but not gone. I could have spent days with the body, getting used to it, loving it, saying goodbye to it. Then again, some part of me was terrified it would change and decay and that part wanted it gone. Her hands weren't moving at all and they were so solid, so hers. There was the wedding ring, the long flat nails. *I'm going to miss her hands,* I thought, my throat tightening. I had an idea: *I'll just take her hands and keep them.* For a minute that seemed a real solution.

So when the men came and took her pulse and said they would remove the body I was glad, too. It was as if by removing the body we could remove the pain, the reality, and move on to the next day. Maybe tomorrow she could come back— *I fooled you!*—and walk down the stairs again. They walked heavily around the house. I remember them wearing white T-shirts and canvas jackets and being tall but that is all. Hello, they said, solemnly. We suggest that you say your farewells and then go upstairs. Some family members find it upsetting to see the body removed.

In a daze, I said goodbye. I kissed my mother's forehead— waxy, the way it had been for days now—and pushed her black hair back. I took a pair of scissors and cut off a lock for myself, then another, for my father. My brothers took one too. Then I kissed her again and said: You were very brave, and I love you.

I fled the room, dutifully going upstairs and hiding my eyes in my pillow, as if I were a child. It was a strange reversal of Christmas: Here we were, at the end of the day, moving back upstairs, averting our eyes, waiting not for the arrival of gifts but for the removal of a gift, the gift of our mother, her body.

At the time the speedy removal felt natural, perhaps because I had no idea what to expect. Now, however, there is a blankness at the center of it that troubles me. We're too squeamish for the ritualistic act of cleansing and purifying, the washing of the body, that used to take place in other times, and still does, in other places, but I wonder if it might have helped me to take care one last time of the body I'd cared about for my entire life.

In early December, I began to experience a strange phenomenon. After my mother's death, I fell into a pattern of waking up twenty or thirty minutes after I'd fallen asleep, covered in sweat, shaking with terror. Of late, though, when I startled awake, I was not panicked, but I had the distinct sensation that *I had no hands*. My arms just ended. Eventually, as I lay there, I could imagine my hands again, and move them, and lift one to the other. I suppose it is a metaphor for my loss: by now, grief is not a fever, it's an amputation. Also, my hands look like my mother's.

SHORTLY BEFORE THREE, we got in our cars to head to the beach. My brothers came with me, leaving Dad to drive alone, which he seemed to want. The route was the same one where my mother had taught me to drive, heading toward the train station, and it was odd to be taking it on my own now.

The beach was windy and gray clouds pressed low to the horizon as we climbed the pass into the sand. Our father was carrying a small gift bag emblazoned with the words MERRY CHRISTMAS. He let Huck off the leash and the dog bounded in joyous circles, not knowing where to go first. Inside the gift bag was a ziplock bag my father was fiddling with. There were the ashes. We shuffled toward the water.

"OK," he said, opening the plastic bag.

"We should do it now if we're going to do it," I said. A family of three was coming down the beach. I didn't want to greet them with handfuls of ash. *Hello! Merry Christmas! We are scattering a dead body on the beach, in the water, amidst your day of joy! Hello! Hello!* And what would they say? *Good luck with your mother! We wish you well! Good luck, farewell!* No, no.

"It's windy," Liam said. "We should get close to the water. Otherwise it's going to be *The Big Lebowski* all over again."

"What's *The Big Lebowski*?" my dad asked. We started explaining the Coen brothers movie; Steve Buscemi's character dies, and Jeff Bridges and John Goodman have to scatter his ashes at a cliff, but the wind comes up and their friend's ashes blow back all over them. The ashes! All over them! Terrible to imagine.

"We don't want that," Dad said.

Liam bent over the slate-gray water and scattered some poinsettia leaves and holly he had gathered from the house before we left. He'd said he wanted something to look at when we put the ashes in, to mark the place. "Otherwise the ashes will just sink. And now these will be with her. She loved these plants."

We were in unknown territory, each of us making up our own rituals. I'd picked out the opening of Keats's "Endymion" to read. The wind loud in our ears, we huddled around, and I read:

A thing of beauty is a joy for ever:
Its loveliness increases; it will never

Pass into nothingness; but still will keep
A bower quiet for us, and a sleep
Full of sweet dreams, and health, and quiet breathing.
Therefore, on every morrow, are we wreathing
A flowery band to bind us to the earth,
Spite of despondence, of the inhuman dearth
Of noble natures, of the gloomy days,
Of all the unhealthy and o'er-darken'd ways
Made for our searching: yes, in spite of all,
Some shape of beauty moves away the pall
From our dark spirits. Such the sun, the moon,
Trees old and young, sprouting a shady boon
For simple sheep; and such are daffodils
With the green world they live in; and clear rills
That for themselves a cooling covert make
'Gainst the hot season; the mid-forest brake,
Rich with a sprinkling of fair musk-rose blooms:
And such too is the grandeur of the dooms
We have imagined for the mighty dead;
An endless fountain of immortal drink,
Pouring unto us from the heaven's brink.

Then my father unzipped the ziplock bag. There were my mother's ashes.

The body that I had loved lay in a sandwich bag. It was a dark gray—charcoal gray. The ash was extremely fine, far finer than I had expected, except for the shards of bones scattered in it. They were small and variously shaped. I had thought all the bone pieces would be like pebbles. One tiny piece looked like a miniature bone, long and thin, rounder at the ends.

All year I had been nauseated by the thought that my mother's body had been burned and now sat in a container somewhere in our house. It was unacceptable. I could accept her death, but I couldn't accept the belated fact of her body—the remains. Now they were in my hands and it was as if someone had poured flammable liquid in my arteries. I felt queer and cold and hot all at once.

Leaning out, I spoke a prayer to my mother, a prayer of safety. I didn't know what I meant. The wind was strong and the ashes landed limply and nonheroically at the ocean's edge. But the water was vast and dark. I thought again of safety.

My brothers had taken handfuls. Eamon's eyes were swollen and red. He walked down the beach and squatted by the water's edge. He carefully placed—even patted—the ashes into the water, as if he were stroking my mother's head for a last time. Atomized, we threw the ashes in handfuls, together, alone, a constellation. I wanted to scatter some further out; taking a deep breath, I cast my hand up and out—just as a gust of wind came and blew the ashes all over Eamon.

"Meg!" he said.

His black parka was covered in gray grit.

"I have some in my mouth—*pfft*," he said.

"Oh no, I'm sorry. I'm sorry. I wasn't trying to Big Lebowski you."

"You Big Lebowski'd me!" he said. "I am *covered*."

"I'm so sorry," I said.

"It's OK."

He walked away. Later my father told me he'd looked over and seen Eamon weeping, and he'd walked down to put his arms around him. "You OK?" he asked.

"I'm fine," Eamon said. "I just have Mom in my eyes."

When we got home, I was extremely hungry and terribly sad and tired. I went upstairs and lay down. I did not dream.

When I woke, we all had a glass of wine together. My head was thick and cottony. "I need to go home," I said to my brothers. As they got their bags, I sat with my father and asked him how he was feeling.

"I feel OK," he said, looking up from his chair. His eyes were bright. "I think it was an important thing to do, especially for you guys. You know, the Egyptians thought there were two kinds of time, one linear, and one cyclical, one ritualistic, one everyday. After a death, everyday time easily returns to take over and rule your life. It's one of the reasons they had so many rituals, I'm now realizing, to deal with the dead—it was to push back everyday time and make space for contemplation of the cosmic. When you do something like this, you step outside of everyday time for a moment, and that's good." He paused, looking off to the side the way he does when he is thinking.

"You do this, and it just feels real—it's part of real life, too. There's wind, it's messy. And you realize you can't avoid the Big Lebowski effect."

I laughed.

"I was saying to Liam in the car on the way home that it's funny: You could wait for the day of perfect weather, for blue sky and warm sun, but then where are you? When does that day come, and why? And what is it once it does come? It made more sense to do it today, even in the bitter cold. And boy, was it cold, my hands were burning. But it's what it was."

As we drove to Brooklyn, Liam told us that after scattering the ashes, my father had spoken to him about how anxious he'd been about the holiday.

"He told me that he woke up in the middle of the night, flashing on the orange flip-flops he got Eamon, and thinking, 'He's going to think I'm so stupid. They're going to seem dorky.'"

Tears came to my eyes at the thought of my father waking, restless, because he was trying on a role that he had never played before.

I looked at Eamon in the rearview mirror. "Call Dad and tell him how much you liked your gifts, especially the orange flip-flops."

Both my brothers groaned.

"No!" Liam said. "That won't help. He'll know I told you."

"Yeah, really," Eamon said. "Come on, Meg."

The elaborate artifice of the funeral home business repulsed my mother, and it repulses me for all the ways it cynically preys on the neediness of the freshly bereaved. "What did you have in mind? Inhumement, entombment, inurnment, immurement? Some people lately have preferred ensarcophagusment," says a funeral adviser at Whispering Glades, in Evelyn Waugh's *The Loved One*, a satire of the funeral business in America. "Well, I think we better just have him buried," responds the hapless British nephew there to perform what he had mistakenly thought was a straightforward duty for his uncle. No: first he must decide whether to get the merely "moisture-proof" Silent Night casket or to splurge for the "dampness-proof" Emperor model.

I was glad my mother chose to be cremated. She wanted to be scattered in many places so she could remain in the world with the kind of expansive, uncentered love she had for it. But I've started to be sorrowful that there is no well-marked place to go to be with her. A few weeks before Christmas, I had a dream about a body in a lot that no one had buried. Waking up, I thought: We need a place to put her, by a lilac bush or a weeping cherry. Liam called that same week and said, "I'm starting to feel that the frustrating thing about cremation is that I'm really wishing there were a place I could be with Mom's body, a place to think about her."

Before we scattered the ashes, I had an eerie experience. I went for a short run. I hate running in the cold, but after so much time indoors in the dead of winter I was filled with exuberance. I ran lightly through the stripped, bare woods, past my favorite house, poised on a high hill, and turned back, flying up the road, turning left. In the last stretch I picked up the pace, the air crisp, and I felt myself float up off the ground. The world became greenish. The brightness of the snow and the trees intensified. I was almost giddy. Behind the bright flat horizon of the treescape, I understood, were worlds beyond our everyday perceptions. My mother was out there, inaccessible to me, but indelible. The blood moved along my veins and the snow and trees shimmered in greenish light. Suffused with joy, I stopped stock-still in the road, feeling like a player in a drama I didn't understand and didn't need to. Then I sprinted up the driveway and opened the door and as the heat rushed out the clarity dropped away.

I'd had an intuition like this once before, as a child in Vermont. I was walking from the house to open the gate to the driveway. It was fall. As I put my hand on the gate, the world went ablaze, as bright as the autumn leaves, and I lifted out of myself and understood that I was part of a magnificent book. What I knew as "life" was a thin version of something larger, the pages of which had all been written. What I would do, how I would live—it was already known. I stood there with a kind of peace humming in my blood.

CHAPTER FIFTEEN

the new year

On December 30, I went to a party at my friend Stephanie's, a reunion of friends. Maureen, a woman I had met earlier this year, took my hand and said, "I've been thinking about you, how are you?" She seems always to be saying what she believes, or finding a way to say what she believes, and so I told her about the ashes, about the difficulty of the anniversary period, and idly mentioned a quarrel I'd had with a friend.

Maureen said, "These are the eighteen months when you find out who can really go there and who can't. This is a vulgar way of putting it, and there are many wonderful things about our culture, but I'm sorry, it is a phobic culture. People do not want to confront the existential mess that is life. They want to check things off—OK, you're OK. And just because you can talk about your grief, you know," she said, looking sharply at me, "doesn't mean you are in control of it, or that you know what's going on. You are in the ocean. And what you think, what you analyze, that is just the descanting of that ocean. Your mind is an ocean and it has scary things in it. While you may be able to analyze your grief at three p.m., that has nothing to do with how you feel at three a.m., in the dark center of night."

Listening to her, I realized that I had been on some level confusing speech—or language—with feeling all year. I had thought, If only I can speak about this, I can understand it, or contain it. But language is the epiphenomenon of a phenomenon that is like waves. The waves aren't the whole of it. They are a small part of a larger entity.

The moment when I flash upon my mother's smile and face and realize she is dead, I experience the same lurch, the same confusion, the same sense of impossibility. A year ago collapses into yesterday in these moments. Periodically for the rest of my life, my mother's death will seem like it took place yesterday.

O N S U N D A Y after New Year's, I drove to New Jersey through bitter cold and high winds and got to my aunt's house in Holmdel just as my grandmother was walking up the driveway, picking her way over the hard ground. She wore thick baby-blue sweatpants and a matching blue jacket, and somehow the optimistic orderliness of her outfit made me sad. The pastels were like children's clothes. What must it be like to be eighty-two and have outlived your grown daughter?

I had made plans to scatter my mother's ashes today with her family. When I'd told my aunt Joanne that my dad, brothers, and I were going to scatter ashes on Christmas, she wrote to say my grandmother would like to have a place to visit my mother. "She keeps saying to me, 'I just need to know *where* Barbara is, to have a place to think of her,'" Joanne wrote. I was embarrassed that I hadn't thought of this earlier.

Joanne and my grandmother had come up with a plan to bury the ashes at a spot near a bridle path on a horse farm where my mother used to go riding. It was now preserved land. Liam and Eamon had gone out of town, and my father decided he couldn't face another ceremony, so I went by myself, reflecting—as I drove—on the odd fact that we lived in a world where a mother might have to ask if she could be part of her daughter's interment ceremony. (The other night I saw a friend; we talked about her father's death, and what her family had done with the body, and she said, "I felt like we made a lot of mistakes. We never invited his siblings to scatter the ashes, partly because we were so focused on just getting our stepmother there, to the house. But can you imagine not being invited to scatter your sibling's ashes?" and she smiled ruefully. "We did the same," I said. "I felt awful.")

Usually, you step inside a Kelly family party and hear loud laughter and the blender busy making margaritas. This time, there were quiet hugs; on the table, fixings for sandwiches were laid out. As we mingled, my grandmother pulled me over and asked, "Are the ashes in a container, like a plain box?"

"Actually, they're in a Christmas bag," I said. "My father put them in a bag for us; let me get it." So I took the bag—a gold "Merry Christmas" bag, with shiny ribbon painted on—and set it on the sideboard. "There. She's eating with us." I couldn't tell if my grandmother was appalled or not.

Over lunch, my grandmother and I sat together and she talked about e-mail. She'd recently gotten an account. Her screen name is BigMamu. "They dragged me kicking and screaming into the twenty-first century, but here I am! Honey," she continued, genially, "take this bag. It's got your Christmas presents." Shit, I thought. We hadn't gotten her anything. My mother always went in on something with her sisters. None of us had thought to do that. We were bad grandchildren! But she was still talking, about the gift, a throw of some kind. "It reminded me of your mother," she said. I was puzzled. A throw? But she continued, and I understood—"It says 'Joy' and it has an angel embroidered on it."

My grandmother rarely talks about her hardships. I have never heard her complain about anything. Last year at the funeral she had said, "I know Barbara's with Jesus Christ." But I could see how hard-won that conviction was. As Joanne passed the dessert around, my aunt Janet and I chitchatted about movies. My grandmother remembered how the last time they all saw my mother, she had been reminiscing about the way her old dog Duchess used to pull her around the neighborhood on her bike. "She'd just get on her bike and off Duchess would run," Grandma said, smiling. "One day Duchess took off after a squirrel and Barbara tumbled off her bike, and she really hurt herself." She paused and looked down at her hands. "I remember that. Barbara really hurt herself that day."

There was much back-and-forth about routes to the farm—*But that way would be a half-hour slower!* Joanne exclaimed to Mary Ellen.

"Can I have a spoon?" my grandmother asked over my aunts, who paid no attention. "Joanne, will you please get me a spoon to bring with us?"

"You want a *spoon*? So you don't have to touch the ashes?" Joanne said. "I think it's OK to touch them. It's *Barbara*, for Christ's sake."

"It is the windiest day," Jackie said. "I got up this morning and said to Nick, 'Today's the day we're spreading Barbara's ashes,' and the wind howled. He said, 'With any luck, she'll just end up back in our yard.'"

We milled in the hall, bundling up. As we walked through the living room, Grandma picked up a throw and said, "See"— and she pointed to a robed angel blowing a trumpet—"this is the angel. That's Barbara. Though I don't know if she's playing a trumpet. Or maybe she's learned," she mused, "and now she's showing off."

She turned to me and said, "That Barbara. She could do anything she put her mind to. I didn't even know her. She had such a quick mind. When she was a little girl, she was always off playing quietly. And I'd say, 'What are you doing, Barbara?' and she'd say, 'Nothing, Mom.' What was going on in that mind? It was impossible to know. Did *you* know her?" She peered at me.

What could I say?

"Don't forget the ashes!" someone called out.

"That would be perfect!" Mary Ellen said. "Barbara would be laughing: *You bunch of idiots are standing out in the cold, and here I am back in the toasty house.*"

The plan got disrupted from the start: Mary Ellen set off on her own route, not Joanne's. The snow was coming down hard.

"They know each other so well," my grandmother said. "Those girls know when to argue and when to agree and then do what they want to anyway."

"Your mother was the master of that," Jackie said, looking at me in the rearview mirror. "It's like she said that day in the hospital: 'It's simple. I know what *no* means. And so when I say no, people listen to me.' She said that was the secret to her life."

Suddenly I knew where we were. It was the road we used to take to go to my dad's parents' house. We passed their street and went on, over a bridge, up a hill, and took a left on a dirt road, passing skeleton trees and a red horse farm.

"You're going to like this spot," my grandmother said, looking back. "It's a big evergreen by an overlook. Horses go by, and you can see the water. In the morning, the river glistens like a million tiny diamonds in the sun. This is a good day for us to do this. She was a winter baby, an Aquarius, like you. I would bundle her up in her snowsuit and out she'd go and come back hours later."

"I'm glad it's snowing," Joanne exclaimed, as we piled out of the cars, the snow swirling around us. "It makes it special. You know it snowed, last year on her birthday, February third, and now it's snowing today, as we put her ashes to rest, on January third. I think it is her way of saying she's with us."

Uncle Nick raised an eyebrow. "Amazing what will happen," he said. "Snow in winter! A miracle!"

"Let me have my magical thinking!" Joanne protested.

We walked down a path high on a hill to the wooden walkway.

"See, you can see the water," Joanne said.

"And this is a horse path," Jackie added. "So horses will come by her all day long in spring and summer." They started down the path.

My grandmother lingered. I went to take her arm and walk with her.

"I know you miss your mom," she said, looking down at her feet. "And that's OK. I miss your grandpa. For years, I missed him all the time."

"Do you still miss him?" I said.

"Yes," she said quietly. "Mostly I'm just sorry about everything he doesn't get to see and do."

My grandfather had died before I was born. But to her, he was still a complete and total presence, or, rather, absence. Just as my mother would be, should I ever have children: an absence I thought about all the time.

The observation deck was small, with a bench and a striking view of the river—a shining circle of ice in the distance—and the farm and trees below. Next to the deck was a robust evergreen, tall, but not as tall as it would get.

"See? That's the tree," Grandma said. "Isn't it pretty?"

And it was.

"I have a prayer to say," she said, as we all took our places by the tree.

My grandmother read a prayer for my mother's soul, leaning over the railing, my cousin Lindsay by her side. Then Joanne read a poem my grandmother had picked out, Henry Wadsworth Longfellow's "A Psalm of Life," which I had never read before. I imagined that my grandmother took the end of the poem as a kind of road map for her own mourning:

> Lives of great men all remind us
> We can make our lives sublime,
> And, departing, leave behind us
> Footprints on the sands of time;
>
>
> Footprints, that perhaps another,
> Sailing o'er life's solemn main,
> A forlorn and shipwrecked brother,
> Seeing, shall take heart again.

Let us, then, be up and doing,
 With a heart for any fate;
Still achieving, still pursuing,
 Learn to labor and to wait.

We stood in a moment of silence. I held up the bag.

"You go," Joanne said.

"No, today is for you."

"Oldest to youngest," one sister said.

Joanne took off her gloves and plunged her hand in the ashes. She knelt in the ground, where one of the husbands had dug up some dirt, and said, "I love you, Barbara, and I think about you every day."

Jackie and Janet both had tears in their eyes as they bent down. Mary Ellen took a handful and let them go, saying, gently, "Rest in peace, Barbara."

I walked back to the cars with my grandmother. I had two different sensations: first, that this was really real, and my mother was *really* dead, and second, that the ceremony felt like a performance from someone else's life, and we'd get home, and there my mother would stand in the kitchen, my mother, like normal.

The snow was truly flurrying now. It was eerie and witchy out and the sadness in my heart grew more swollen, but it was the swell of mystery: What strange beauty surrounds us, and how impermanent our vision of it, how palpable our loss when those we love no longer can view the world they would adore.

"That was good. We scattered her ashes and she has a place to be." She paused, and added, with typical Kelly deflection, "And now we're all going to get pneumonia."

W HEN I GOT home that night, I called my dad. "They found a beautiful spot," I said, "one that Mom would have liked. It's near where you grew up—right by Grandma and Grandpa's house, just off Navesink River Road, above a horse farm."

"You know what?" Dad said slowly. "This is really crazy. But when Mom and I first met, and no one knew we were together, that's where we would go. We'd park, and we'd sit under a great big tree. We used to call it the farm. We'd say, 'Let's go to the farm.' We'd just go to this tree, and we'd sit there and talk for hours. We'd go there and be alone and smoke pot." Dad laughed. "It was the summer before we got married. I was a dopey first-year teacher. Mom was still a high school student. All that stuff wasn't there—it wasn't a public park. The people who owned the farm never said anything to us." He broke off. "Where was the tree again? Do you drive down and go over a tiny bridge, and then take a left?" he asked.

"Yes. I'm looking here at the map again. It's called 'Browns Dock Road.'"

"That's it," he said. "We had this tree we'd sit under, and we would look down at the river."

He pauses, thinking. "That makes me glad I didn't go today," he says. "Because I would have been like, 'Holy shit, this is where we used to go smoke pot before you knew we were together!'" He sounded young and amused when he said that, the father I remember from my childhood.

CHAPTER SIXTEEN

so that nothing was lost and nothing ever went away

On my mother's second birthday since her death I found myself calculating: She was two in death years, fifty-seven otherwise. Last year I had forgotten it was her birthday, remembering only after returning from work. It had been five weeks since she had died. When I got home and saw the date—with a knife-twist of pain—I read Tennyson's memorial for his friend Arthur Henry Hallam:

Break, break, break,
On thy cold grey stones, O Sea!
And I would that my tongue could utter
The thoughts that arise in me.

O, well for the fisherman's boy,
That he shouts with his sister at play!
O, well for the sailor lad,
That he sings in his boat on the bay!
And the stately ships go on
To their haven under the hill;
But O for the touch of a vanished hand,
And the sound of a voice that is still!
Break, break, break,
At the foot of thy crags, O Sea!
But the tender grace of a day that is dead
Will never come back to me.

That idea of the grace of a "day that is dead," a grace I'd too often taken for granted, haunted me. How could I have failed to appreciate that I still lived a life before loss?

Now I wondered if forgetting my mother's birthday last year was a form of self-protection. This year, the eight-day period between my birthday and my mother's birthday was excruciating. I felt unreasonably angry. I was cold all the time. A winter chill had settled over New York—but it was more than that. I felt cold all the time. One day, as I walked down the street, having wrapped a big black scarf up over my nose, I passed a man who joked, "It's not that cold, honey."

I really wanted to punch him. It's not cold for you, asshole.

People kept saying to me, "It gets better at a year, doesn't it?" Or, "I hear it gets better at a year." It did. It got "better" in that I could go for days without thinking too much about the fact that someone I still loved as dearly as I ever did was dead. But to expect grief to heal is to imagine that it is possible to stop loving, to reconcile yourself to the fact that the lost one is somewhere else. So *heal* isn't the right word. I love C. S. Lewis's metaphor: A loss is like an amputation. If the blood doesn't stop gushing soon after the operation, then you will die. To survive means, by definition, that the blood has stopped. But the amputation is still there. (Complicated grief, it seemed to me, was more like an amputation that wouldn't stop bleeding, threatening your very survival; I could understand why therapists have wanted to designate it as a psychiatric disorder in the *DSM-V*, though it made me nervous that more people would just think of grief as something that ought to be treated by doctors, rather than supported by everyone.)

Her birthday, of course, was one of the days she had told me she would miss, that afternoon in the hospital when we talked about her death. I'd planned to spend the night with my father and my brothers in Connecticut. My car got towed in the afternoon and I spent an hour and a half trying to find it and get it out of the lot while snow flurries came down. I got home at seven at night, exhausted, frustrated by the stress of dealing with city government bureaucracy—on this, of all days?—and I didn't drive up, as planned. Guilt hovered around me, as if I had failed my mother. She had made the point of telling me how she would miss her birthday. And here I had gone and missed it. Perhaps I had given up on her too soon in the hospital. Perhaps if I had not "prepared" myself for her death, she would still be here. That night, a terrible pain struck my hip, and I lay sleeplessly in pain.

At one point earlier that day, an image of my mother in the hot tub at Isabel's—the hot tub used to help with her pain—had flashed into my brain. When memories you haven't thought of since the death first come up, they hurt. But I kept finding that it hurt less to remember things a second time. I think this is why people always say that it gets better after a year—even though after a year you're not *done* with mourning, you have cycled through the seasons, through holidays, family rituals, living through them for the first time without the person who's gone. And in this sense I've come to feel that Freud's description from "Mourning and Melancholia" is somewhat accurate, however programmatic it seems: you do go through the memories and alter them, because now they've been accessed in the context of separation. Of course, certain memories remain particularly vivid—whenever I remember them they feel like razor icicles, burning my mind.

Once asleep, I had weird tangled dreams and woke with a headache. Resolving to try to move forward, I wrote on my computer: *This little period is now behind us.* Only I mistyped it: This little period is *not* behind us.

I'd never before considered the closeness of "not" and "now."

My mother is not now.

But she was, and she is now, in the minds of those who remember her: her smile, her voice, her little intonations, her smell—all in us.

IN THE SUMMERS when we used to go canoe camping for a week or two on Moosehead Lake, we would drive up from New York City in a station wagon packed to the brim with boxes and bags and two canoes precariously strapped to the top of the car. My brother and I were each allowed to bring a "crate"—a wooden wine box—of books. "One crate," my mother said firmly. I would line my crate carefully with paperbacks, rearranging to get everything in. Once, after the long drive without air-conditioning—our cars, the cast-offs of friends, never had such niceties—my dog jumped out an open window when my parents stopped to get our camping license. "Finn!" I cried in fright, thinking he'd finally had enough of us. But all he did was shoot down the hill to the dock and then jump straight out into the blue water. He had never seen a lake before.

The lake was huge, stretching lakily out to the horizon, and it changed you to see it, after the hours of asphalt and the car climbing huge hills and descending them, climbing again and descending, hemmed in by hundred-year-old oaks and maples. When you got to the shoreline and saw the trees curving away over the water you felt free. I would open the tent, insert the flexible metal wires that gave it shape, and hammer in the supporting pegs with a rock or a book, my brother doing the same, his blond head bent over a peg. He was young and slower than I was and I'd shove him aside in the end to do it myself. Then we got inside and read. I read *The Scarlet Pimpernel* by flashlight one night when I was ten. It all seemed exciting and dastardly and terrifying; the ground was rotting under me as I read. How could these people want to murder lords and ladies? Lords and ladies were the heroines of my storybooks. I didn't understand how the book took for granted these casual dealings in blood and terror. I found it terrifying to learn that this had been real. I remember my confusion, the night pressing against the tent, and the mahogany light cast by the flashlight against the yellowing book. Now all those books have yellowed; they sit on the rec-room bookshelves in my dad's house, some moth-eaten and mildewed, others brittle, the corners of the pages breaking as you turn them.

In the morning we paddled out, I with my father, my brother with my mother, each with a dog and packs and crates of books in the center of the canoe. Finn and Jesse (my mother's German shepherd) didn't like to settle in the canoe; they'd stand wagging their tails, startling as the canoe tipped. "Down!" my father would say sternly. They would lie down and then we paddled for what felt like hours. First you'd set out for a point that seemed impossibly distant. Then you would get there. Then you would paddle around that point and paddle to another impossibly distant point. Finally you would stop and make camp, setting up the tent. Usually, if we found a spot we liked, with good swimming, we'd stay a few days, reading and swimming all day long, cooking dinner on our little "convection oven" at night—usually some kind of baked beans, Spam, and brown bread. On these trips, and only on these trips, my brother and I were allowed to drink Kool-Aid, which we'd make from mix packets. There was a panoply of flavors and we lingered over them in the supermarket, savoring the idea of each exotic new one, like Lemon-Lime and Watermelon-Cherry.

Every summer we went—three or four summers, I can't remember—my brother and I begged to get to Fox Island. It was a remote spot with a great rock about twenty feet out from the shore. You could climb on the rock and read, or you could use it for diving. I liked to swim out there with my mother and practice diving. I wanted to be a great diver or gymnast. My mother encouraged me in this; she was athletic and tensile and elegant in the water and she'd watch my brother and me jump and do flips with as much interest as if we were performing miraculous jackknives, when in fact we were just tipping downward off the rock with our legs piked.

In the morning my mother used the solar water shower—a big black plastic jug, designed to absorb the sun's heat and be hung on a tree—to shave her legs. I used to hover near her and watch. Why are you doing that? I remember asking.

To get the hair off my legs, she said.

Can I do it?

No.

Why not?

You don't need to.

But I have hair on my legs.

Little girls don't need to.

And I went away and threw some rocks in the water and watched her over my shoulder: a woman, bending in the sunlight, taking the hair from her legs.

After she died, we were going through boxes of memorabilia she kept about each of us—typically disorganized. One of the things I found was a card I made her on her birthday when I was about six:

TO MOM

I LOVE YOU.

I LOVE THE STORIES

YOU MAKE WITH ME.

I LIKE THE BED YOU

MADE FOR MY DOLL HOUSE.

I HAVE A GOOD TIME

WITH YOU. YOUR A GOOD MOM.

YOUR A GOOD SEWER.

HOW COME YOU ARE SO

NICE. AND HAPPY

BIRTHDAY.

How come you are so nice. I think I really wanted to know.

In that moment, my mother's death is a flat thing, impossible to accept. The spring after she died, my father sent me this passage, by a scholar of ancient Egypt:

> We usually think of time as a river, a river like the Nile, with strong, swift current bearing us further and further away from what we have been and towards the time when we will be not at all. . . . But perhaps we should think of time as a deep, still pool rather than a fast-flowing river. . . . Instead of looking back at time, we could look down into it . . . and now again different features of the past—different sights and sounds and voices and dreams—would rise to the surface: rise and subside, and the deep pool would hold them all, so that nothing was lost and nothing ever went away.

The passage consoles me. The idea of time as a pool brings an actual solace, conjuring up the peculiar fact that our brains so often make the past as vivid as the present, without our choosing. Our memory is our weather, and we are re-created by it every day.

CHAPTER SEVENTEEN

hasten slowly

Mostly I don't believe much in an afterworld, but I find myself thinking a lot about the notion that we have some kind of after-being—if not after-consciousness. And maybe after-being is a consolation. Certainly my mother seemed to find it so. In those last days she seemed to be looking across a barrier, into a space I couldn't see, couldn't imagine. She talked about wanting to look at old things. Once when I drove her home from chemo two springs ago—in the months she was intuiting for the first time that this cancer was the thing that would kill her—she wanted me to take her to the Cloisters. I had a hard time looking at her because her skin was so gray. We walked through the colonnade—like an old monastery—and studied the art. This has been in the world for so long, she said. See how carefully it was made. In the sun, emerging from the dark, limping because her knee hurt, she bent to the herbs and flowers just coming up—lupine, myrtle, columbine. Here comes the spring, she said, as if she knew she would never see it again. Later, I would sit next to her, rubbing her feet, watching her look out the window—she looked past us, like an X-ray machine. Already left behind, I was angry at moments, wanting to call out: Come back! Come back! But my desire felt obscene. It was clearly wrong—spiritually wrong. It denied nature. And nature is, as far as I can tell, spirit.

When my mother was dying, I prayed for the first time in my life, and the world returned something to me: a vibrational awakening, a gift of energy that loosened the snake grip of pain and, blessedly, also shook me out of the numbing anger settling in my brain. Later I read Virginia Woolf's aborted memoir, *Moments of Being*, and was drawn to a passage recalling the paralyzing shocks that sent her into a depression, and how her experience of imperilment and recuperation through writing led her to conclude that there is an order behind our existence:

> From this I reach what I might call a philosophy; at any rate it is a constant idea of mine; that behind the cotton wool is hidden a pattern; that we—I mean all human beings—are connected with this; that the whole world is a work of art; that we are parts of the work of art. . . . Certainly and emphatically there is no God; we are the words; we are the music; we are

the thing itself. And I see this when I have a shock. . . .

There is a pattern hid behind the cotton wool.

This is the closest description I have ever come across to what I feel to be my experience. I suspect a pattern behind the wool, even the wool of grief; the pattern may not lead to heaven or the survival of my consciousness—frankly I don't think it does—but that it is *there* somehow in our neurons and synapses is evident to me. We are not transparent to ourselves. Our longings are like thick curtains stirring in the wind. We give them names. What I do not know is this: Does that otherness—that sense of an impossibly *real* universe larger than our ability to understand it—mean that there is meaning around us?

Time does now feel like what Madeleine L'Engle calls, in *A Wrinkle in Time*, a tesseract. L'Engle describes it as being akin to when your skirt folds, and two disparate places in the fabric suddenly touch. A memory reaches out and touches my mind and I live proximate to it all day long—talking, writing, working, hearing my mother's voice saying, "Here comes the spring." And I will keep hearing her voice every spring until I, too, see my last spring.

SITTING HERE among my precarious stacks of books about death and grief, trying to get "a handle" on what this loss means, trying to collect the information and set it all down, I am struck suddenly by the ridiculousness of my endeavor. I have felt that, as Flaubert wrote, "language is like a cracked kettle on which we beat out tunes for bears to dance to, while all the time we long to move the stars to pity." But life is out there in the world, in the hum of enterprise, flirtation, engagement, watching a sunrise, the sand under your feet, and the green in your eyes; life is in the moths fluttering up at dusk into the candle flames on a porch in summer.

I sit here in my tiny study, bills dropped on the floor, books piling by the desk—*Death and Western Thought, Death's Door, The Denial of Death, This Republic of Suffering*—believing in some primitive part of my brain that if I read them all, if I learn everything there is to know, I'll solve the problem. I will find the answer to the equation. And when I look up from my dutiful work, my head bowed to the page, there will be my mother again, saying, *Good night, Meg,* from the door, the dog at her heels, her hair loose around her face, her eyes that were so particular, so *hers*—there she will be.

Where is she?

She is gone, and I will be, too, one day. I wake to my warm room, the wind roaring outside and the sun just coming up on another ordinary Tuesday when I will teach my class and go out to get coffee and eat some salad for lunch. But all the while my brain will be preoccupied by the question of death. And that makes it hard, at times, to pay my bills or pay attention to concerns of this world.

I can't find the information I want in all these books. Not even in the Bible, which sits there, too, a fat red tome full of old wisdom. And that is my answer: I need to walk in the streets, through the bracing, chill air, to know it, to feel it, because it cannot be merely *thought* about.

Later, I go to an engagement party and dance with a friend, the little blades in my heart clicking, shuffling, quieting.

Iᴛ ʜᴀs ʙᴇᴇɴ fifteen months and one week since my mother died. A year, three months, a week.

Tomorrow, it will be a year, three months, a week, a day. And so forth. What can I say? There is nothing "fixed" about my grief. I don't have the same sense that I'm sinking into the ground with every step I take. But there aren't any "conclusions" I can come to, other than personal ones. The irony is, my restored calm is itself the delusion. I'm more at peace because that old false sense of the continuity of life has returned.

I have learned a lot about how humans think about death. But it hasn't necessarily taught me more about my dead, where she is, what she is. When I held her body in my hands and it was just black ash, I felt no connection to it, but I tell myself perhaps it is enough to still be matter, to go into the ground and be "remixed" into some new part of the living culture, a new organic matter. Perhaps there is some solace in this continued existence.

When I was talking to my father about my mother's decision to be cremated, one spring night after dinner, sitting at the kitchen island, drinking wine together, he said, "She just kept saying, 'I don't want to be buried in the ground,' and she said, 'I want to be everywhere.' And I brought up the fact that you kids might want to have a place to visit, to be with her—I thought of that. But 'I don't want to be buried in the ground' is all she would say." He paused and drank some wine. Every time I looked at him I had the impression of a streak of white paint disappearing into a colorfully painted wall. It was almost as if he couldn't focus on us, or I couldn't focus on him. His eyes were walled and melting at once, circles dripping down under them into his face. "Knowing your mother, I would think she thought there was something sad about cemeteries. Sure, a grave is a place where we can go remember the dead when we want to, and that is important. But the rest of the time the grave just stands there unlooked after, segregated from the living, and you're there alone with all the other dead." He stroked his beard, like the professor that he is. "She would have thought that was sad," he said.

"I can see that," I said. "I can see that she would've wanted to be like the Whitman version of the dead, all underfoot." I was thinking of the lines from the end of "Song of Myself": "I bequeath myself to the dirt to grow from the grass I love, / If you want me again look for me under your boot-soles." One never has the impression that Whitman means look for him under your boot-soles *in the cemetery*; he means in the living world.

"Exactly," my father said. He rubbed his eyes. They were red and full and watering.

Once upon a time, there was a little girl who stayed too long in the bath. Her mother warned her that she would wrinkle up like a raisin and go down the drain. She looked at the whorls of her fingers, puckered and pink. When she looked up, her mother had left the room. Mother? she called, and called again. The fluffy white towel had fallen to the ground. She heard nothing. She stood up and pulled the towel from the ground. And pink from the heat, she stepped out of the bath at last and into the cool and shocking air.

In the second spring since my mother died, the tiny furled buds are appearing once more on the trees. Seeds have sprouted. The daffodils are coming up. Walking down the street near my apartment, I pass the house where I lived when I was two and three. My first memories are from this house—my socks being scrabbled, the dream of the parade, my mother holding me up to look out the window on a scrubbed gray day like this one. The tree branches swung close to our second-floor window. On their spidery fingers bulged green pods. I asked what they were.

Those? Those are buds, she said. Do you see their green tips? Those will grow bigger and unfurl into leaves and then the trees will be all green like last summer. They grow in spring.

And she explained the cycle of seasons to me—that it had been winter, and would be summer, and that this happened every year.

It is fitting—it is cyclically fitting—that my mother should disappear from this planet before I do. I know she would prefer it that way. It is fitting, too, that one day as the winter gave way to spring I woke up to realize that I wanted to feel pleasure—that I missed reveling in the world.

Perhaps it is fitting, too, that while my grief has lessened, my sense of being motherless has intensified. I hadn't anticipated this. The first grips of grief were so terrible that I couldn't wait to get beyond them, to a state I hoped might be "better." But as each new day arrives I find myself, though suffering less acutely, feeling *more* unmothered. Strange. I have a piercing sense of empathy for friends who lost a parent when they were young. Even at my age, I still have so many questions, about children, about cooking, about what my mother thought of her life's work.

One thing that helps is summoning up her words and her jokes—even her little rebukes; when I get annoyed by something trivial, I catch myself saying (often out loud) the very refrain of hers that used to so irritate me: "Lighten up, Meg." In fact, I have begun to feel my mother *inside* me—usually on holidays or in groups. My brothers have more of her blithe and freewheeling spirit. But lately there are these moments when it's as if her spirit enters and inhabits me; it's palpable, like being possessed. The word *inspiration* comes from the Latin preposition *in* and the verb for "to breathe," *spirare* (which also gives us our word "spirit"). Perhaps I have breathed my mother in. It is true that the other day, as I was driving to work, someone cut me off; I rolled down my window and called out into the air, "You asshole," just as she used to.

On Easter, Isabel and Diana and their families came over

to my father's, and I went too. I found myself making a little joke that I thought my mother would've liked over dinner. I hid Easter eggs with Diana for her three young sons. The chaos of life suddenly seemed more absurd than it ever had—for example, when the dog started eating the Easter egg I'd thought I'd cunningly placed behind the barbecue. (A week later, I was having dinner with an old friend who lost her father almost ten years ago. I asked her how her life had changed following his death. She paused and thought. "Mostly, the world seems funnier," she said.) That weekend both Isabel and Diana said that at moments I had reminded them of my mother. *If only,* I thought. Then I thought, *If so, it's not my doing, it's hers.*

I think about my mother every day, but not as concertedly as I used to. She crosses my mind like a spring cardinal that flies past the edge of your eye: startling, luminous, lovely, gone. A holiday—even something like Mother's Day, a holiday she hated—always leads me to remember her, to think about what she is missing, what I am missing. This Easter, I think about all the things I never said along the way, about how much her example meant to me, about the way she never let the perfect be the enemy of the good, and nearly always made a joke out of the situation.

The bond between a mother and child is so unlike any other that it is categorically irreplaceable. *Unmothered* is not a word in my dictionary, but I often find myself thinking it should be. The "real" word most like it—it never escapes me—is *unmoored.* The irreplaceability is what becomes stronger—and stranger—as the months pass: Am I really she who has woken up again without a mother? Yes, I am. Some nights I still lie awake, nerves jangled, in the velvet dark, staring out the window, listening to the cars pass by like echoes of other lives lived, not lived, my breath shallow, my toes cold, my mind drifting in the shallows and currents of the past, like a child wading in a stream.

With my mother's death the person who brought me into the world left it, a portal closing behind her, a line of knowledge binding her body to mine in the old ways. Who else contained me, felt me kick, nursed me, held the towel out to me when I got out of the bath, age thirteen, the last time she helped me bathe. I remember, because she had wanted to come in and wrap me in the towel and I was resisting it. When she did, holding up the sheet of white cloth, she said, "You're growing breasts, Meg," and then—and God, it made me so uncomfortable at the time—"They're pretty." Who else do I share this history with? No one. Because she is not here, I must mother myself.

We were with her when she died, her breath deepening, the oxygen machine wheezing, making more noise than anything in the house, her skin going yellow, pebbly, her body numbingly diminished. And there she was, breathing, still breathing, and when her breath changed and the hospice worker came to take her pulse and her blood pressure, he turned to us and he said, "The only thing keeping her alive right now is her heart." And of course it was her heart keeping her alive, moving the blood, causing her to sing to us from her coma all that morning as we unwrapped presents as we always have and always will until we do not. It was heart that moved her and heart that led us to gather by her and give witness to the breath rasping and pressing forward as it is designed to do. In the beginning there was the wind, the wind made by breath, the word of the wind, and in our hearts we kept telling the story over and over of how we loved her and were there, there, there, once we were all there, and she took a breath like a gasp and her eyes opened and she took us in, all of us there, and then she breathed once more, the last breath, and we were there and she was not, and even now I think, Come on, Mom, stay another night, stay the night—

Stay the night.

acknowledgments

I would like to thank Eleanor Chai and Andrew Beer for their support and friendship, without which this book would not have been written; Jerome Groopman, whose remarkable generosity and expertise helped me and my family through my mother's illness; Carin Besser, Henry Finder, Dana Goodyear, Katie Kitamura, Cressida Leyshon, Jodie Morse, Michael Specter, Darin Strauss, and Julia Turner for taking the time to read my work and offer their editorial insight; Ann Hulbert, and Katie Roiphe, for first encouraging me to write about grief; David Remnick, David Plotz, and Jacob Weisberg, for publishing sections of this book in *The New Yorker* and *Slate*; Chris Calhoun and my editor, Megan Lynch, for their invaluable wisdom and support; and my father and my brothers and James Surowiecki, my family: lights along the way.

a note on further reading

I read many books and poems in the year after my mother died, in the hopes of better understanding my experience. Not all the books I consulted are mentioned in the text. Nevertheless, the following books informed aspects of both my intellectual and my emotional experiences of grief, and I am indebted to them. Because my reading was guided by emotion, I took a highly subjective and idiosyncratic approach, and, needless to say, this list is not comprehensive. I hope it will be of use to those looking to understand more about loss.

Critical Studies and Nonfiction

Ariès, Philippe. *The Hour of Our Death: The Classic History of Western Attitudes Toward Death over the Last One Thousand Years.* Trans. Helen Weaver. New York: Vintage, 1987.

_____. *Western Attitudes Toward Death: From the Middle Ages to the Present.* Trans. Patricia M. Ranum. Baltimore: John Hopkins University Press, 1974.

Barthes, Roland. *Camera Lucida: Reflections on Photography.* Trans. Richard Howard. New York: Hill &Wang, 1981.

Becker, Ernest. *The Denial of Death.* New York: The Free Press, 1973.

Edelman, Hope. *Motherless Daughters: The Legacy of Loss.* New York: Delta, 1994.

Enright, D. J., ed. *The Oxford Book of Death.* Oxford: Oxford University Press, 1983.

Faust, Drew Gilpin. *This Republic of Suffering: Death and the American Civil War.* New York: Alfred A. Knopf, 2008.

Foucault, Michel. *The Birth of the Clinic: An Archaeology of Medical Perception.* Trans. A. M. Sheridan Smith. New York: Pantheon, 1973.

Gehlek Rimpoche. *Good Life, Good Death: Tibetan Wisdom on Reincarnation.* New York: Riverhead, 2001.

Gilbert, Sandra. *Death's Door: Modern Dying and the Ways We Grieve.* New York: W. W. Norton, 2006.

Gill, Derek. *Quest: The Life of Elisabeth Kübler-Ross.* New York: Harper & Row, 1980.

Gorer, Geoffrey. *Death, Grief, and Mourning in Contemporary Britian.* London: The Cresset Press, 1965.

Groopman, Jerome. *The Anatomy of Hope: How People Prevail in the Face of Illness.* New York: Random House, 2005.

Harrison, Robert Pogue. *The Dominion of the Dead*. Chicago: University of Chicago Press, 2003.

Nuland, Sherwin. *How We Die: Reflections on Life's Final Chapter*. New York: Alfred A. Knopf, 1994.

Rich, Adrienne. *Of Woman Born: Motherhood as Experience and Institution*. New York: W. W. Norton, 1976.

Sogyal Rinpoche. *The Tibetan Book of Living and Dying*. New York: HarperOne, 2002.

On the Psychology of Grief

Bonanno, George A. *The Other Side of Sadness: What the New Science of Bereavement Tells Us About Life After Loss*. New York: Basic Books, 2009.

Bowlby, John. *Loss: Sadness and Depression (Attachment and Loss)*. New York: Basic Books, 1982.

Freud, Sigmund. "Mourning and Melancholia," in *General Psychological Theory: Theories on Paranoia, Masochism, Repression, Melancholia, the Unconscious, the Libido, and Other Aspects of the Human Psyche*. Ed. Philip Rieff. New York: Collier Books, 1963.

Kübler-Ross, Elisabeth. *On Death and Dying*. New York: Macmillan, 1976.

———, ed. *Death: The Final Stage of Growth*. New York: Touchstone, 1975.

———, and David Kessler. *On Grief and Grieving: Finding the Meaning of Grief Through the Five Stages of Loss*. New York: Touchstone, 2005.

Leader, Darian. *The New Black: Mourning, Melancholia and Depression*. London: Hamish Hamilton, 2008.

Lewis, Thomas, et al. *A General Theory of Love*. New York: Random House, 2000.

Martin, Terry L., and Kenneth J. Doka. *Men Don't Cry . . . Women Do: Transcending Gender Stereotypes of Grief*. London: Taylor & Francis, 2000.

Parkes, Colin Murray. *Bereavement: Studies of Grief in Adult Life*. New York: International Universities Press, 1972.

————. *Love and Loss: The Roots of Grief and Its Complications*. New York: Routledge, 2009.

Rando, Therese A. *How to Go On Living When Someone You Love Dies*. New York: Bantam, 1991.

Studies

Horowitz, Mardi J., et al. "Diagnostic Criteria for Complicated Grief Disorder." *Focus* 1 (2003), 290–298.

Lindemann, Erich. "Symptomatology and Management of Acute Grief." *American Journal of Psychiatry* 101 (1944), 141–148.

Prigerson, Holly G., and Paul K. Maciejewski. "Grief and Acceptance as Opposite Sides of the Same Coin: Setting a Research Agenda to Study Peaceful Acceptance of Loss." *British Journal of Psychiatry* 193 (2008), 435–437.

Fiction, Poetry, and Drama

Davis, Lydia. "Head, Heart," in *Collected Stories*. New York: Farrar, Straus & Giroux, 2010.

Eggers, Dave. *A Heartbreaking Work of Staggering Genius*. New York: Simon & Schuster, 2000.

Gilbert, Sandra. *Inventions of Farewell*. New York: W. W. Norton, 2001.

Gordan, Mary. *Final Payments*. New York: W. W. Norton, 2001.

Hemingway, Ernest. "Indian Camp," in *In Our Time*. New York: Boni & Liveright, 1925.

Jansson, Tove. *The Summer Book*. Trans. Thomas Teal. New York: New York Review of Books, 2008.

Maxwell, William. *They Came Like Swallows*. New York: Harper & Brothers, 1937.

Proust, Marcel. *Swann's Way*. Trans. C. K. Moncrieff. New York: Vintage, 2009.

Shakespeare, William. *Hamlet*.

Tolstoy, Leo. *The Death of Ivan Ilyich*. Trans. Hugh Aplin. London: Hesperus Classics, 2005.

Washington, Peter, ed. *Poems of Mourning*. New York: Everyman's Library, 1998.

Young, Kevin, ed. *The Art of Losing: Poems of Grief and Healing*. New York: Bloomsbury, 2010.

Memoir

Barnes, Julian *Nothing to Be Frightened Of*. New York: Alfred A. Knopf, 2008.

Barthes, Roland. *Mourning Diary*. Trans. Richard Howard. New York: Farrar, Straus & Giroux, 2010.

Broyard, Anatole. *Intoxicated by My Illness, and Other Writings on Life and Death*. New York: Fawcett/Columbine, 1992.

Didion, Joan. *The Year of Magical Thinking*. New York: Alfred A. Knopf, 2005.

Dillard, Annie. *Holy the Firm*. New York: Harper & Row, 1977.

Ehrlich, Gretel. *The Solace of Open Spaces*. New York: Viking Penguin, 1985.

Fitzgerald, F. Scott. "The Crack-Up," in *The Crack-Up*, ed. Edmund Wilson. New York: New Directions, 1956.

Gornick, Vivian. *Fierce Attachments*. New York: Farrar, Straus & Giroux, 1987.

Jamison, Kay Redfield. *Nothing Was the Same*. New York: Alfred A. Knopf, 2009.

Lewis, C. S. *A Grief Observed*. New York: Harper & Row, 1961.

Manguso, Sarah. *The Two Kinds of Decay*. New York: Farrar, Straus & Giroux, 2008.

Quindlen, Anna. *Living Out Loud*. New York: Ballantine, 2004.

Rieff, David. *Swimming in a Sea of Death: A Son's Memoir*. New York: Simon & Schuster, 2008.

Romm, Robin. *The Mercy Papers: A Memoir of Three Weeks*. New York: Scribner, 2009.

Roth, Philip *Patrimony: A True Story*. New York: Simon & Schuster, 1991.

Strayed, Cheryl. "The Love of My Life," in *The Sun*, September 2002; and in *The Best American Essays 2003*. Ed. Anne Fadiman. Boston: Mariner, 2003.

Styron, William. *Darkness Visible: A Memoir of Madness*. New York: Vintage, 1992.

Wieseltier, Leon. *Kaddish*. New York: Alfred A. Knopf, 1998.

Williams, Marjorie. "Hit by Lightning: A Cancer Memoir," in *The Woman at the Washington Zoo: Writings on Politics, Family, and Fate*. Ed. Tim Noah. New York: Public Affairs, 2006.

Woolf, Virginia. *Moments of Being*. New York: Harcourt, 1985.

CRAZY AGE

Jane Miller

'Ever since I have inhabited old age, I have looked and listened,
mostly in vain, for news of what it is like for others who inhabit
it too. Naturally, I'm interested in its well-known depredations,
the physical and mental ones that people in their forties and fifties
so publicly dread. And who would not delight in the theatrical
props of old age – the pills and sticks, the shrieking hearing aids
and the tricks for countering the loss of names and threads
and glasses. But that's not all. I have a fond hope that in old age
there may be new kinds of time and of pleasure, perhaps even new
kinds of vitality, and that, though we forget and muddle and
fail to hear things, there may be moments when we truly
understand what's going on for the first time. But then
I've always been a late developer.'

Deeply thoughtful, wry and resilient, this fascinating and
absorbing book about growing older is a life-enhancing
look at what all of us – if we are lucky – can aspire to.

'Jane Miller's writing is so fluid and amusing . . .
If anyone doubts that old age can actually be interesting,
this is the book for them'
Katharine Whitehorn, *Observer*

978-0-84408-649-8

EVERY SECRET THING

My Family, My Country

Gillian Slovo

A passionate witness to the colossal upheaval that has transformed her native South Africa, Gillian Slovo has written a memoir that is far more than a story of her own life.

For she is the daughter of Joe Slovo and Ruth First, South Africa's pioneering anti-apartheid white activists, a daughter who always had to come second to political commitment. While recalling the extraordinary events which surrounded her family's persecution and exile, and reconstructing the truth of her parents' relationship and her own turbulent childhood, Gillian Slovo has also created an astonishing portrait of a courageous, beautiful mother and a father of integrity and stoicism.

'A luminous achievement'
Observer

'Gillian Slovo has written a brave book, as unsparing of herself as it is of her parents . . . a moving testimony'
Christopher Hope, *Independent*

978-0-84408-599-6